OECD
ECONOMIC
SURVEYS

1999-2000

AUSTRALIA

ORGANISATION FOR ECONOMIC CO-OPERATION AND DEVELOPMENT

ORGANISATION FOR ECONOMIC CO-OPERATION AND DEVELOPMENT

Publié également en français.

Table of contents

•••••

Tables

Figures

BASIC STATISTICS OF AUSTRALIA

THE LAND

Area (1 000 sq. km)	7 682.3	Population of major cities, 30 July 1997 (1 000):	
Agricultural area, 1986-87, per cent of total	61	Sydney	3 935
Urban population, 1991, per cent of total	85	Melbourne	3 322
		Brisbane	1 548
		Perth	1 319
		Adelaide	1 083

THE PEOPLE

Population, March 1999 (1 000)	18 918	Civilian employment, 1998 (1 000)	8 553
Number of inhabitants per sq. km	2.4	of which: Agriculture	421
Natural increase, 1998 (1 000)	121	Industry [1]	1 869
Net migration, 1998 (1 000)	112	Other activities	6 263

PARLIAMENT AND GOVERNMENT

Composition of Parliament following latest elections:

Party	Senate	House of Representatives
Australian Democrats	7	–
Australian Labor Party	29	49
Independent	1	5
Greens	2	–
Liberal Party of Australia	31	75
National Party of Australia	5	18
Country Liberal Party	1	1
Total	76	148

Present government: Liberal/National Party coalition
Next general elections for House of Representatives: October 2001

PRODUCTION

Gross domestic product, 1998		Gross fixed capital formation, 1998	
(A$ million)	579 111	Percentage of GDP	23.8

GENERAL GOVERNMENT SECTOR, PER CENT OF GDP, 1998

Current disbursement	32.0	Current revenue	35.2
Current transfers	13.9	of which: Direct taxes	17.8

FOREIGN TRADE

Main exports, 1998, per cent of total:		Main imports, 1998, per cent of total:	
Food, beverages and tobacco	18.3	Food, beverages and tobacco	4.4
Raw materials	20.1	Raw materials	1.7
Fuels	17.0	Fuels	4.4
Machinery and transport equipment	12.0	Machinery and transport equipment	45.9
Other manufactured products	32.5	Other manufactured products	43.7

THE CURRENCY

Monetary unit: Australian dollar	Currency unit per US dollar, average of daily figures:	
	Year 1998	1.5923
	October 1999	1.5347

1. Including mining, electricity, gas and water, and construction.

This Survey is based on the Secretariat's study prepared for the annual review of Australia by the Economic and Development Review Committee on 10 November 1999.

•

After revisions in the light of discussions during the review, final approval of the Survey for publication was given by the Committee on 25 November 1999.

•

The previous Survey of Australia was issued in December 1998.

Assessment and recommendations

*Strong economic
growth,
an improving
labour market
performance and
low inflation...*

The performance of the Australian economy since the onset of the East Asian currency and banking crisis in July 1997 has exceeded most expectations. Real GDP grew by 4½ per cent in fiscal year 1998-99, only slightly slower than the year before and substantially above its trend rate of some 3½ per cent over the past thirty years. By mid-1999, the current expansion had entered its ninth year, making it the longest upswing since the 1960s. It was accompanied by robust employment growth, a substantial reduction in unemployment, a pick-up in trend productivity and much lower inflation than experienced at any time since the early 1960s, factors which underpin the sustainability of the current expansion. However, the unavoidable negative effects on export demand of the weaker regional and global environment, the deterioration in Australia's terms of trade from falling world commodity prices and strong import growth induced by robust domestic demand led to a widening current external deficit, which rose to 5.5 per cent of GDP as a whole for 1998-99 and around 6 per cent of GDP by mid-1999.

*... based on
a judicious mix
of sound
macroeconomic
and structural
policies...*

The robustness of domestic demand at the time when the Asian crisis became apparent is an important factor which helped the Australian economy to overcome the negative impact on growth of the contraction of many of its major export markets. The basis for the continuation of the strong domestic demand had been laid by a judicious mix of sound macroeconomic and structural policies, which *inter alia* had brought inflation under control, reduced public sector borrowing and generated an acceleration of productivity growth. High rates of productivity growth have allowed substantial increases in real wages to be reconciled with broadly flat unit labour costs. These have underpinned price stability from the labour cost side while at the same time strengthening the purchasing power of households. Price stability and financial market reform have made credit readily available to the private sector at low interest rates, supporting both household consumption and private investment. Consumer spending was further encouraged by capital gains from rising house and share prices, boosted by the decline in interest rates since early 1995, with various measures of private saving declining somewhat.

... helped to cope with the Asian economic crisis and the global slowdown of economic activity

The steep fall in world commodity prices which followed the weakening of global demand after the outbreak of the Asian crisis put downward pressure on the Australian dollar exchange rate. But the persisting low inflation environment allowed the economy to absorb the exchange rate depreciation and its potential inflationary effects without compromising the medium-term inflation target. The exchange rate depreciation stabilised export prices in Australian dollars and improved Australia's international price competitiveness, allowing exports to be diverted to more prosperous regions of the world, in particular the United States and Europe. The depreciation also tended to support import-competing sectors, limiting the adverse effect of the global downturn on economic activity. The negative impact on the current external account was contained further by increased government savings as a result of fiscal consolidation. Model simulations confirm the substantial contribution made to the favourable macroeconomic performance during the Asian crisis by the particular combination of expansionary monetary policy and fiscal retrenchment adopted by the authorities.

Economic growth is projected to slow...

Mainly on account of a declining rate of stock building and weakening fixed investment, especially in the mining sector, economic growth is projected to slow to around 4 per cent in 1999. These factors and a decline in private consumption growth contribute to a further slowing in economic growth in 2000, to around 3 per cent. Business investment should begin to rise again in 2001 as the rundown in mining investment slows, pushing economic growth back up to around 4 per cent. Growth in activity around these rates should support continuing strong growth in employment, resulting in a reduction in the (year-average) unemployment rate to around 6½ per cent in 2001. This decline in the unemployment rate could result in some small rise in wage pressures. At the same time, international recovery, especially in Asia, should result in firmer prices for imported goods and services in the consumer price index (CPI). Together, these factors underpin a small rise in underlying inflation to around 2½ per cent in 2001. Headline inflation, however, will rise considerably more owing to the introduction of the tax package in July 2000. This is assumed to add 2¾ percentage points to the price level in the year after its introduction. The improved outlook for the international economy should strengthen export growth and Australia's terms of trade, cutting the external current account deficit to around 4¼ per cent of GDP in 2001.

... but there are both domestic and external risks

A major upside risk to these projections is that private consumption expenditure may not slow by much if households continue to enjoy large capital gains on housing and, to a lesser extent, on equities. This could encourage households to go on borrowing to finance growth in consumer expenditures in excess of disposable incomes. Another domestic risk is that the introduction of the goods and services tax (GST) in July 2000 could raise underlying inflation expectations owing to the difficulty of distinguishing GST-related price increases from underlying inflation. This could increase wage demands and make consumers less resistant to rising prices although the effects should be offset by the income tax cuts and other compensation measures. Although the outlook for the international economy has improved markedly in recent months, there are still some significant risks. In particular, a sharp decline in the US stock market could result in a much harder landing than assumed, cutting growth across the globe. There is also the risk that Asian countries may not complete the structural reforms that are necessary to improve the functioning of their capital markets, with the result that the recent burst of growth could be short-lived. This would undercut Australia's export performance and terms of trade, delaying progress in reducing the external current account deficit until the domestic economy slowed further.

Expansionary monetary conditions have supported economic growth

Economic growth has been supported by the expansionary monetary conditions of the past year or so, in spite of some real effective appreciation of the Australian dollar since late 1998. This is the more so given the sharp competition between financial intermediaries which has resulted in a continued narrowing of interest rate margins and has entailed a further downward drift in major indicators of the real cost of credit in 1999.

Monetary conditions are set to prolong the economic expansion, but the authorities will need to remain vigilant to contain inflation in the medium term

Now that the Asian crisis is largely over, and given that there has been some increase in medium-term inflation risks, a readjustment of monetary policy to a less expansionary setting has been considered appropriate. Hence, the Australian cash rate, which had remained at 4¾ per cent since the cut in December 1998, was increased by 25 basis points on 3 November 1999, in response to an improving external trading environment and the likelihood that the slowing in growth of GDP in Australia would be milder and less protracted than originally expected. The general challenge facing monetary policy over the year ahead will be to assess the extent to which the policy setting currently prevailing remains appropriate as circumstances change. Growth is projected to be sufficient to generate further declines in unemployment over the year ahead. The authorities will need to remain vigilant to the risk that medium-term inflation pressures may increase further given the overall strength of the economy. Another risk is that of second-round effects flowing from the GST. The Reserve Bank has indicated that it will abstract from the initial price-level impact of the GST, but it will be important to ensure that this one-off price-level impact is not incorporated into ongoing inflation.

Progress in budget consolidation should be preserved

In view of Australia's large current account deficit and with monetary conditions supportive of growth, it is appropriate that fiscal policy remains geared to preserving the budget consolidation achieved in recent years. Adjusting for one-off factors, the general government underlying cash surplus is officially forecast to rise in fiscal year 1999-2000 by 0.5 percentage point of GDP to 0.8 per cent of GDP, despite economic growth falling below trend. However, Australia's involvement in East Timor, which was not anticipated when the Budget forecasts were made, will reduce somewhat this rise in the budget surplus if not fully offset by additional measures. The introduction of the tax package in the following year (fiscal year 2000-01), at a budget cost of A$ 6.9 billion (1 per cent of GDP), offsets the consolidation that would otherwise have occurred, resulting in a small decline in the general government underlying cash surplus. This seems a reasonable price to pay for the long-term benefits of a more efficient tax system. Fiscal policy settings imply modest, but rising budget surpluses in subsequent years, notably for the Commonwealth government. Given the maturity of the present upswing, such policy settings would appear to be consistent with the Commonwealth government's medium-term objective of achieving budget balance over the business cycle. The medium-term framework should help to limit the risks of fiscal slippage over the period ahead. It will be particularly important that such slippage does not occur if Australia is to maintain its present sound fiscal position especially as experience has shown that large swings in budget balances can occur over the business cycle.

The introduction of accrual budgeting reinforces arrangements for prudent fiscal management

The Commonwealth government has also made further progress in the past year in establishing an institutional framework more supportive of ongoing prudent fiscal management. This reform process began with the Charter of Budget Honesty, which requires the government to lay out its medium-term fiscal strategy and short-term objectives in each budget, with both the strategy and objectives being based on principles of sound fiscal management, as set out in the Charter. The other major element of fiscal reform, accrual budgeting, came into effect with the 1999-2000 Budget. Accrual budgeting provides a more accurate view of the total activity of government and its long-term effects, supporting the principles of sustainability and sound fiscal management expressed in the Charter. The move to accrual budgeting is also a vital element of reforms aimed at achieving better value from public expenditures. For the first time, the full cost of providing public services will be apparent and managers will be held accountable for the performance of their agencies in contributing to the achievement of government objectives. It will also be easier to compare the costs of internal provision of services with the cost of outsourcing. With these reforms, fiscal institutions in Australia represent best practice in terms of assuring prudent and efficient fiscal management.

A flexible, decentralised industrial relations system gradually replaces the prescriptive, centrally-determined awards...

Achieving more flexible labour market regulations to enhance the economy's adaptability to external shocks and a changing economic environment has been a priority of recent Australian governments. A major step in this direction was the implementation of the Workplace Relations Act 1996 (WRA) at the beginning of 1997, which reduced the role of centrally-determined awards in Australian industrial relations and promoted the bargaining of wages and employment conditions at the enterprise level. The WRA limited the formerly comprehensive coverage of awards to 20 "allowable matters" as from 1 July 1998, designed to confine the role of the award system to a safety net of minimum wages and core conditions of work. These, and other changes being made to awards through the simplification process, are making awards less comprehensive and prescriptive. But given the enormous complexity of the old system and the legal uncertainties of the parties about award simplification, the move to the new regime has proved to be a rather slow process, although decisions by the AIRC have assisted this process and it appears to be accelerating. And even though those awards which have been simplified impose fewer constraints on the operation of enterprises than before, the rather extensive coverage of the 20 "allowable matters" still implies some degree of complexity. Hence, regulatory flexibility of workplaces could be enhanced if the number of "allowable matters" were reduced further and their definitions and specifications tightened so as to provide a less comprehensive set of core conditions of employment. In this regard, the Government in June 1999 sought to enhance the regulatory flexibility of workplaces by proposing changes to the WRA to advance award simplification. Under these proposals, the definitions and specifications of the various allowable award matters would be tightened and the number of allowable matters would be reduced by removing elements which duplicate other legislative entitlements or are more appropriately decided at the workplace level. These changes, if approved, would clarify the original intent of the WRA, widen the scope for better quality and more innovative agreement-making and require the individual situation of the respective enterprise to be properly taken into account.

... but the move to enterprise bargaining is slow and needs to be supported by the States

Progress has also been registered in promoting the spread of collective – and to a lesser extent – individual agreements at the enterprise level. But given the evolutionary approach to industrial relations reform, comprehensive agreements that determine all work conditions and pay requirements and completely replace awards are not yet widespread. In spite of their recent fast take-up rate, albeit from a low level, comprehensive enterprise agreements continue to cover a relatively small share of employees, estimated at less than 10 per cent. In fact, a large number of enterprise agreements retain links with existing awards. Many agreements deal only with a relatively narrow range of work conditions, although the key issues in the workplace relationship are generally covered by agreements. Hence, in order to move more quickly towards comprehensive and innovative agreements at the enterprise level, the Government proposed in June 1999 to simplify the regulatory requirements in the WRA for the formalisation of collective and individual agreements. The current Government has also restored a co-operative working relationship with State industrial relations systems, although more still needs to be done to achieve a nationally coherent workplace relations framework so as to reduce costs for governments and businesses. In this regard, discussion is underway on the use by the Commonwealth of its powers under the Australian Constitution for regulating corporations to underpin a unified workplace relations framework in Australia.

A new competitive market for employment assistance offers more choices for jobseekers

Following the announcement in the 1996-97 Commonwealth Budget, a new competitive market for employment services came into effect in May 1998. At the heart of the reform is the introduction of the *Job Network*, which is a contestable employment placement market, with full competition between private, community and government contracted service providers and *Employment National*, a corporatised government employment services agency. Competition encourages a high level of service, and fees paid to Job Network organisations provide a strong incentive for them to perform. To ensure that highly disadvantaged jobseekers benefit from the assistance provided by Job Network, a differential fee structure applies with the highest fees being paid for those who are most at risk and hardest to place in a job and being paid in full only after a jobseeker has been off allowances for longer than six months. Although a final assessment has to wait until the results of a comprehensive evaluation are available in late 2001, early results are encouraging, in terms of outcomes achieved by clients.

The mutual obligation principle aims at integrating young unemployed in a work environment...

In July 1998, the Government introduced its Mutual Obligation initiative for jobseekers aged 18-24 years on unemployment payments for six months. The initiative is guided by the principle that it is fair and reasonable to ask unemployed people to participate in an activity which both helps to improve their employability and makes a contribution to the community in return for payments of unemployment benefits. Young jobseekers are required to participate in an approved activity in addition to job search over a six-month period. Activities include Work for the Dole which was introduced in November 1997. This programme seeks to involve young jobseekers in a work environment and to foster appropriate work habits. Participants must work 24-30 hours per fortnight for six months, depending on their age, which allows them to both acquire work skills and continue search for a job. In 1999, Work for the Dole has been extended to young people who complete year 12 at school and who have received Youth Allowance for at least three months. Mutual obligation was also extended to 25-34 year olds who have received unemployment benefits for 12 months and the Work for the Dole programme expanded to accommodate those in this older group who are on the full rate of unemployment payment.

... but a careful evaluation is needed

Whether the mutual obligation programmes represent a successful shift away from passive income support to more active labour market policy depends on the extent to which programme participants are provided with work experience and skills valuable enough to make them attractive to employers as potential employees. The requirement under Work for the Dole that programme-jobs must not compete with paid employment in the regular labour market remains a problem as it favours unskilled work with little opportunity for training, which may impede the integration of the unemployed into gainful work. A comprehensive examination of the employment and incentive effects of the scheme will be undertaken as part of an evaluation of mutual obligation.

Education and training continue to be adapted to the requirements of the labour market but early school leavers need more help

The market for training has developed further with the introduction in 1998 of user choice and the strengthening of the institutional framework within which it operates. While the growth in structured vocational training is encouraging, more could be done to improve the integration of the vocational education and training system with broad education sectors. Many early school leavers remain at considerable risk of being locked into marginal labour market activities that may not lead to better skills and employment prospects. More needs to be done to reduce the incidence of early school leaving. Curriculum reforms to make school more relevant and useful for potential early school leavers, as planned in New South Wales, would help, as would better co-operation between Technical and Further Education (TAFE) colleges and high schools.

The National Competition Policy is giving impetus and coherence to structural reforms

Developments in global markets, reinforced by reductions in import protection, have led not only to pressure for reform in labour markets and in education and training, but also in the infrastructure industries, which were dominated by Government Business Enterprises, and in product markets more generally. The National Competition Policy (NCP), agreed between governments in 1995, extended competitive conduct rules to all businesses, including Government Business Enterprises, set out competition principles and established a framework for implementing the NCP. The NCP has provided a coherent framework for reforms already underway in the major infrastructure industries as well as providing impetus to complete these reforms. An incentive for State and Territory governments to complete the reforms, most of which are in their domain of responsibility, is that the NCP payments from the Commonwealth government are conditional on satisfactory results. This puts pressure on the lower tiers of government to follow through on structural reforms. Considerable progress has been made in reforming infrastructure industries, and those customers that have gained choice of supplier have enjoyed substantial price cuts, especially for electricity.

Progress needs to be made in implementing competition policy reforms that affect small business

The NCP is also providing impetus to other elements of the structural reform programme by requiring all anti-competitive legislation to be reviewed and to remove regulations that restrict competition unless they are demonstrated to be in the public interest and the objectives of the legislation cannot be obtained in another way. Almost 1 700 separate Acts or Regulations were identified for review. Most of the reviews that have not yet been translated into government reforms affect small businesses, making reform politically difficult. Such reviews include a number of agricultural marketing arrangements, retail trading arrangements, taxi licensing, the regulation of the professions (including retail pharmacy arrangements) and mandatory insurance arrangements. Even though many of these reforms are likely to encounter resistance from the groups that earn rents from these arrangements at the expense of the rest of the community, it is nevertheless important that progress be made in these areas. This will preserve the overall coherence of the NCP, contributing to a more efficient and dynamic economy, and make it clear that there are small returns from investing in lobbying efforts to earn rents through anti-competitive arrangements. Making progress in these areas may require gaining greater political acceptance by providing some form of assistance to those groups bearing significant initial costs and/or by phasing in the reforms.

Tax reform will reduce the economic costs of taxation

An element of structural reform long on the agenda in Australia, tax reform, has finally been agreed and comes into effect in July 2000. The main elements of the reform are the introduction of a 10 per cent Goods and Services Tax (GST) on all consumption items except most health and education, some supplies provided by charities and basic foodstuffs, abolition of the wholesale sales tax and a variety of other indirect taxes (although not all at the same time), and income tax cuts. There are also measures to reduce high effective marginal tax rates. The reform represents a substantial shift away from specific indirect taxes to a general indirect tax, levelling the playing field between different goods and services. In addition, tax revenue security will be better assured by GST than by the indirect taxes that it replaces, which were largely based on the production of goods (rather than services) which are in long-term decline as a share of GDP. Finally, the reductions in marginal income tax rates and marginal effective tax rates will improve work and saving incentives. While the tax reform package represents a substantial improvement over existing arrangements, some of the benefits of reform were lost in the compromise required to get the Senate's approval. An especially unfortunate aspect of the compromise is that the abolition of some harmful State indirect taxes has been delayed. For example, abolition of the tax on bank account debits has been delayed until 2005 at the latest. Once these taxes are abolished, Australia's indirect tax system will be much improved. The government is now working on business tax reform. This is intended to make business taxation more neutral between types of entity and between industries and to reduce the impact of the capital gains tax on capital transfer and mobility and impediments to venture capital investment in Australia.

Economic reforms have contributed to higher productivity growth

The benefits of a comprehensive and consistent approach to structural reform have become apparent in Australia's productivity performance. Since the late 1980s, those sectors displaying the highest total factor productivity (TFP) growth (utilities, finance and insurance, communication services and wholesale trade) have been the focus of major structural reforms. TFP growth has picked up significantly in the latest productivity cycle (1993-94 to 1997-98), to an average of 2.4 per cent per year compared with a long-run average of 1.4 per cent. Capital productivity has turned up particularly sharply, growing by 0.8 per cent per year in the latest productivity cycle compared with a long-term decline. This reflects an improved quality of investment decisions, the shedding of old capital and the more efficient use of existing capital, as would be expected following the kinds of economic reforms made in Australia. The sectors that recorded the greatest improvements in trend labour productivity growth are labour-intensive, suggesting that labour market reforms, which have given firms greater scope to negotiate changes in working arrangements to enhance productivity, may have contributed to this outcome.

Overall, with output growth having been strong, these productivity improvements do not appear to have been at the expense of employment and growth.

To sum up

In summary, Australia has continued to grow above its trend rate over the past two years with the economy proving to be remarkably resilient in the face of significant weakness in many of its trading partners, especially in Asia. At the same time, inflation remained low and the rate of unemployment was reduced further. This performance was helped by dynamic growth of domestic demand at the time when the crisis broke out, and a credible mix of macro-policies which allowed the exchange rate to move freely, kept monetary conditions expansionary and maintained fiscal retrenchment. Although the current account deficit rose to somewhat above 6 per cent of GDP by mid-1999, the cyclical nature of the increase was well understood by financial markets. Economic growth is now projected to slow and export growth to rise, which may cut the current external deficit to around 4¼ per cent in 2001. The authorities will need to remain vigilant to inflationary risks including the risk of one-off price effects associated with the new goods and services tax being incorporated into ongoing inflation. Fiscal policy should remain geared to preserving the budget consolidation achieved in recent years. It is important that fiscal slippage does not occur if Australia is to maintain its present sound fiscal position. Earlier structural reforms, reflected in an acceleration in trend total factor productivity in the 1990s, also helped cushion the impact of the global slowdown. Economic efficiency should be strengthened further and the rate of structural unemployment reduced through the ongoing move to a flexible industrial relations system, the operation of a competitive market for employment assistance and stronger efforts to integrate the young into the labour market. The broad-based implementation of the National Competition Policy and the introduction of a more efficient tax system in July 2000 should help to consolidate the productivity gains that are now being seen. These gains represent the fruits of a consistent and comprehensive set of interacting macroeconomic and structural policies which need to continue to be pursued with rigour through the coming years if this better performance is to be maintained.

I.   Recent trends and short-term prospects

A resilient economy in the face of the Asian crisis

The Australian economy continued to perform impressively over the past twelve months, notwithstanding the recession in Japan and the financial crisis in a number of other East Asian countries, which caused a marked slowdown of world economic growth in 1998 and 1999. Real GDP grew by 4½ per cent in fiscal year[1] (FY) 1998-99, following 4¾ per cent in 1997-98, thus remaining above its average growth rate of some 3½ per cent during the past thirty years. By mid-1999, the current expansion entered its ninth year, making it the longest upswing since the 1960s. Although the economic recovery during the 1980s was stronger and generated more employment (Figure 1), the current expansion has been steadier and is accompanied by much lower inflation. In consequence, the present upswing is likely to be more sustainable: despite some indications that growth could slow somewhat, at present there is no sign that the expansion will come to an end soon. While productivity gains had accounted for a greater proportion of growth than during the 1980s, this upturn has been strong enough to reduce the unemployment rate by some 4 percentage points from its peak to currently around 7 per cent, the lowest rate for nearly a decade. Recent trends are discussed in some more detail further below in this Chapter.

The continuation of the economic expansion since the outbreak of the East Asian currency and banking crisis in July 1997 is most remarkable as Japan and the troubled Asian economies – Korea, Indonesia, Malaysia and Thailand – are important trading partners of Australia; together they absorbed nearly 40 per cent of total merchandise exports during the 1990s. The resilience of the economy[2] in weathering the Asian downturn is largely the result of a judicious mix of sound macroeconomic and structural policies, which brought inflation down to a very low level, strengthened government finances and generated an acceleration in total factor productivity growth. As a consequence of stable prices and financial market reform, credit has become readily available at record-low interest rates since 1997, lending support to both household consumption and private investment. All this put the economy in an excellent position to cope with the consequences of the crisis (Figure 2). The fact that the early stage of the Asian

Figure 1.   **The current expansion compared**

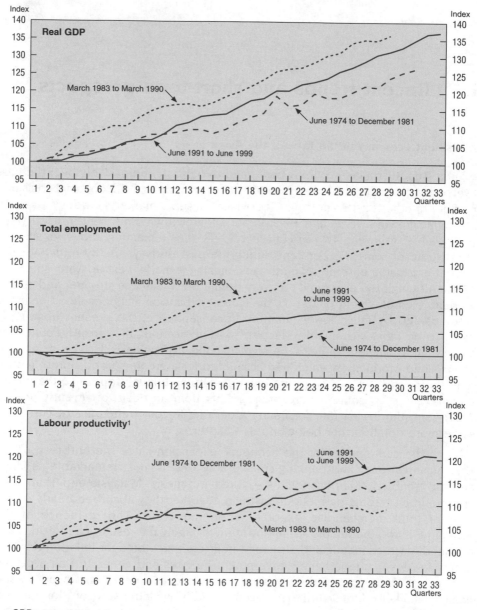

1.   GDP per employee.
Source: Australian Bureau of Statistics and OECD, *Main Economic Indicators.*

Figure 2. **Key aspects of economic activity**

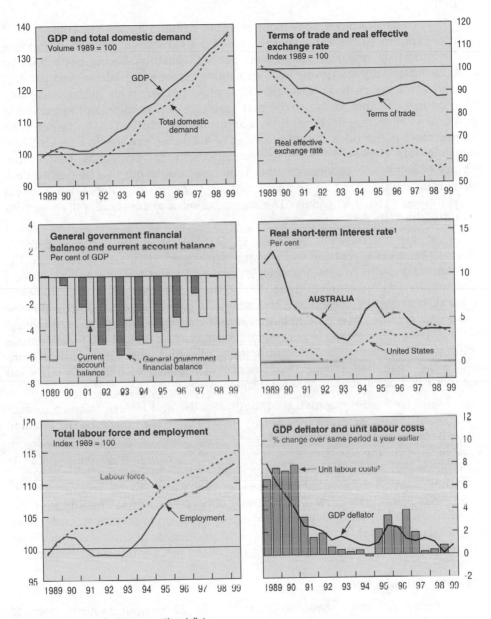

1. Deflated by the private consumption deflator.
2. Non-farm unit labour costs.
Source: Australian Bureau of Statistics and OECD, *Main Economic Indicators.*

meltdown coincided with strong growth of domestic demand in Australia also helped.

The crisis-induced weakening of global demand for raw materials caused world commodity prices to fall steeply, which put substantial downward pressure on the Australian dollar exchange rate. But with inflation having been brought down to historically low levels and with more competitive labour and product markets, the Reserve Bank was able to maintain interest rates unchanged while the economy was able to absorb the exchange rate depreciation and its expected temporary inflation effects without compromising the inflation target. The improvement in the price competitiveness of Australian exports as a result of the exchange rate depreciation assisted substantially in redirecting part of the exports of goods and services to other regions of the world; this helped to limit the contractionary effect of shrinking import demand in major Asian markets on Australian economic activity. The depreciation also lent support to import-competing industries.

It was not possible, however, to entirely avoid the negative demand effects of the weaker regional and global environment. Hence, in spite of success in diverting exports to new markets, Australia's export volume growth slowed substantially and the terms of trade deteriorated. Together with strong domestic demand, both factors contributed to a widening current external deficit. But the *de facto* unavoidable deterioration in the current external account has been limited by the substantial increase in government savings as a result of the fiscal consolidation pursued since 1996. The contributions of sound monetary and fiscal policies to the Australian economy's resilience in the face of the Asian crisis are discussed in more detail in Chapter II below.

The inevitable negative contribution of the real foreign balance to economic growth since the Asian crisis broke out was more than offset by the ongoing strength of domestic demand,[3] private consumption in particular (Table 1). Household spending was boosted *inter alia* by solid growth of real wages and gains in employment. Strong growth of labour (and total factor) productivity in recent years has allowed substantial increases in real wages to be reconciled with broadly flat unit labour costs. This not only underpinned price stability from the labour cost side but was also instrumental in the pick-up in employment demand. Recent trends in total factor productivity and microeconomic reforms which have fostered overall economic efficiency are discussed in Chapter III of this Survey.

Domestic demand

Private consumption remained the main pillar of buoyant domestic demand in FY 1998-99, growing by 4.5 per cent, nearly as strongly as the year before (Figure 3). Household spending again outpaced disposable incomes, so that the long-term trend decline in the household saving ratio[4] continued, to a historically

Table 1. **Demand and output**

Percentage changes, FY 1997-98 prices

	From previous period				From previous period, seasonally adjusted annual rate		
	Calendar years		Fiscal years[1]		1998		1999
	1997	1998	1997-98	1998-99	I	II	I
Consumption							
Private	3.9	4.3	4.9	4.5	3.0	4.7	5.4
Public	1.9	2.7	4.1	2.4	1.6	0.3	7.3
Gross fixed capital formation	11.4	6.1	9.4	4.6	5.2	4.6	3.7
Public sector	0.9	−8.3	−8.5	17.8	−47.1	72.1	−0.2
General government	7.7	2.2	−3.4	8.2	−1.3	25.2	−14.4
Public enterprises	−6.6	−21.3	−15.1	32.1	−98.0	173.8	18.5
Private sector	14.3	9.1	13.5	2.1	16.4	−5.7	4.5
Dwellings[2]	14.4	12.6	15.5	7.4	15.3	6.0	2.3
Other building and structures	8.8	26.4	16.2	−0.9	71.8	−23.5	−10.4
Machine and equipment and intangible fixed assets	17.1	2.1	11.7	1.0	−0.1	−3.8	11.7
Machine and equipment	15.5	−2.2	8.6	−2.7	−6.1	−6.5	8.4
Intangible fixed assets	28.2	27.8	31.0	20.2	34.5	9.1	26.1
Livestock and transfer costs	8.5	2.9	10.4	−0.2	3.3	−6.1	8.6
Livestock	−2.7	3.8	3.5	4.0	0.0	8.0	0.0
Ownership transfer costs	10.8	2.8	11.7	−0.9	3.9	−8.5	10.2
Final domestic demand	5.2	4.4	5.8	4.2	3.3	3.9	5.3
Increase in stocks[3]	−1.6	1.7	0.2	0.7	3.0	−1.0	1.8
Total domestic demand	3.6	6.2	6.0	4.8	6.3	2.8	7.1
Exports of goods and services	11.5	−0.4	3.8	1.7	−2.5	5.9	−2.3
Imports of goods and services	10.3	5.9	9.7	5.0	4.6	3.2	8.6
Change in foreign balance[3]	0.2	−1.3	−1.2	−0.7	−1.5	0.5	−2.3
Statistical discrepancy[3]	0.0	0.2	0.0	0.3	0.2	0.7	−0.3
GDP	3.9	5.1	4.8	4.5	5.0	4.0	4.5
Farm	7.1	8.7	0.9	8.2	7.0	−0.3	27.8
Non-farm	4.2	5.0	4.9	4.4	5.0	3.8	3.9
Memorandum item:							
Business fixed investment[4]	14.3	8.7	12.8	0.4	18.8	−10.0	4.8

1. Fiscal years begin 1 July.
2. Including real estate transfer expenses.
3. Contribution to changes in real GDP (as a percentage of real GDP in the previous year).
4. Excluding investment in public enterprises.
Source: Australian Bureau of Statistics.

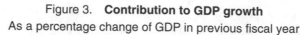

Figure 3. **Contribution to GDP growth**
As a percentage change of GDP in previous fiscal year

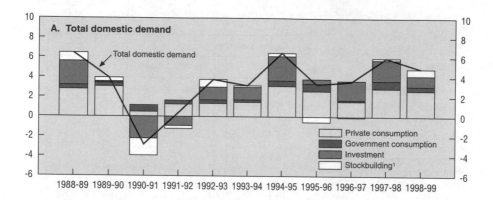

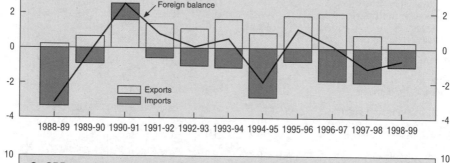

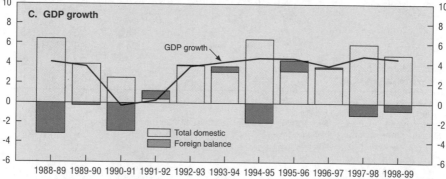

1. Including statistical discrepancy.
Source: Australian Bureau of Statistics, *National Accounts.*

low level of just under 2 per cent of household disposable income in FY 1998-99 (Figure 4). However, gross saving[5] of households has fallen less steeply: it roughly halved over the past two decades, from around 14 per cent to some 7 per cent of GDP in 1998 (Figure 5). Broader measures of the saving behaviour show an even less pronounced decline. For example, gross private saving adjusted for inflation declined from around 20 per cent of GDP twenty years ago to around 15½ per cent of GDP in 1998.

The impact of rising asset prices on household wealth is likely to have contributed heavily to the ongoing decline in the private saving ratio as capital gains tend to encourage consumer spending but are not counted as income in the national accounts. Over the past three years, aggregate household wealth has risen in total by about 35 per cent. An important source of capital gains of households was the steady rise in house prices in recent years – for example, established house prices in Sydney and Melbourne increased by some 6.1 per cent and 10.9 per cent over the year to the June quarter 1999 respectively. Households also enjoyed capital gains from rising share prices (up about 35 per cent over the past four years), especially those of privatised[6] and demutualised[7] companies. At present some 40 per cent of adults hold direct or indirect (via managed funds) investments in the share market, about double the level at the beginning of the decade. The proportion of equities held directly by households and indirectly through life insurance and pension funds are estimated to account for more than one-fourth of total household assets.

The fall in the private saving ratio is consistent with above average consumer confidence[8] in recent years. It was only interrupted by a temporary deterioration in mid-1998, probably reflecting concerns about the effect of world financial market turbulence on the Australian economy. These concerns have given way to incoming good news on the economic front, in particular the edging down of the unemployment rate since mid-1998.

The strength in private consumption has also been encouraged by the low cost of borrowing as a consequence both of the generally low interest rate level and intensified competition between financial intermediaries (see Chapter II below). Moreover, the rise in the value of owner-occupied housing has further increased the availability of home equity loans for non-housing purposes which bear a lower interest charge than unsecured personal borrowing. All this made credit-financed consumption more attractive and has led to soaring credit extended to households (up 15 per cent at an annual rate in the first half of 1999). The strong increase in total credit extended to households has implied a substantial rise in the ratio of household debt to disposable income, which has doubled since the early 1980s to about 94 per cent in mid-1999. It is thus higher than in a number of other OECD countries, though still significantly lower than in the United States, Japan, the United Kingdom and Canada, where household debt

Figure 4. **Household saving ratio**

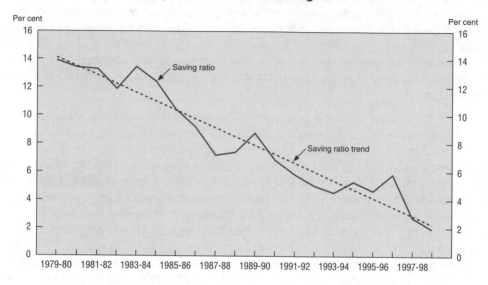

Source: Australian Bureau of Statistics.

Figure 5. **Gross national saving**
Per cent of GDP

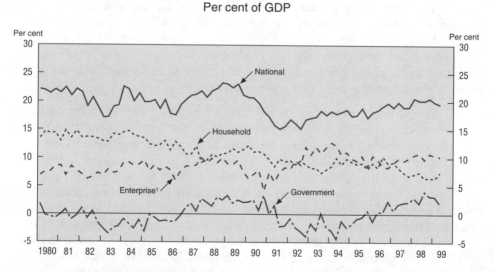

1.   Includes public enterprises and public financial enterprises.
Source: Australian Bureau of Statistics.

Figure 6. **Household debt and debt-servicing burden**
Per cent of household disposable income

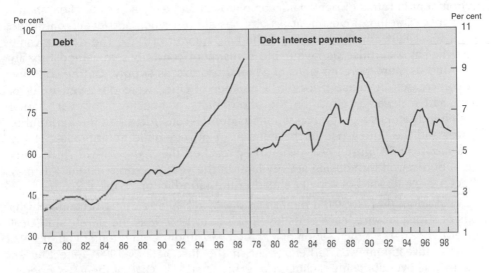

Source: Reserve Bank of Australia.

ranges between 100 and 120 per cent of disposable income. The growth in debt has also been less than the increase in the value of assets, so that net worth has increased rapidly. Given the fall in interest rates on credit in recent years, the ratio of the households' aggregate interest payments to disposable income – the debt-servicing burden – is at a moderate level, about one-third lower than the previous cyclical peak in the late 1980s (Figure 6). Hence, for the time being, household indebtedness should not be a serious constraint on private consumption growth. The run-up in debt has nevertheless raised the exposure of households to the impact of interest rate increases.

The slowing growth of household consumption to a quarterly rate of about 1/2 per cent in the June quarter of 1999 is likely to reflect a correction of the extraordinary growth earlier in the year, in part related to calendar irregularities. Retail sales data for the September quarter of 1999 point to a continuation of solid growth of private consumption volumes. The introduction of the GST on 1 July 2000 is expected to result in some bring-forward of consumption expenditure for some categories and delay expenditure for others. However, it is not clear whether the net effect of these timing changes on consumption expenditure in 1999-2000 will be positive or negative.

Following its recovery from the slump in 1995-96, *residential construction* activity peaked by mid-1998, supported by an unusually favourable investment environment in terms of personal income growth and easy access to cheap housing finance. Dwelling investment activity has slowed since and even contracted – on a seasonally adjusted basis – in the June quarter of 1999. The decline came somewhat as a surprise as favourable investment conditions remained broadly intact and as there were no signs of generalised excess supply. On the contrary, steep increases in house prices in a number of cities were observed in 1998, which had a negative effect on the affordability of housing. However, partial housing indicators suggest a pick-up in residential construction in the September quarter and the strong rise in the number of private building approvals in the three months to August 1999 – when they reached the highest level since early 1995 – bodes well for housing activity later in the year. To some extent, this may reflect a bring-forward of activity ahead of the introduction of the GST.

Business fixed investment peaked in the March quarter 1998, after nearly six years of strong growth. Much of its levelling out in 1997-98 is the purely statistical consequence of the privatisation of a natural gas pipeline[9] in the first half of 1998. Business investment was rather robust in the first half of 1999, reflecting an encouraging overall business climate, a record share[10] in GDP of the gross operating surplus of corporate enterprises of about 15 per cent, and favourable conditions of external funding of investment. It is the result of generally buoyant capital expenditure in sheltered industries on the one hand (examples are construction, property and business services, and communications and accommodation services), which more than compensated for the contracting investment in exposed industries on the other, such as mining and tourism. Weakening mining investment was, however, not only a consequence of contracting export demand and the ensuing fall in commodity prices and profits, but also due to the recent completion of a number of large projects in the fields of base metals, coal and gas. Hence, after an increase in mining investments from 1995 to 1998 by over 50 per cent, it declined by nearly 30 per cent during the three quarters to March 1999. The deferral of investment in projects in the tourism sector is in part a response to the decrease in overseas arrivals from troubled Asian economies during the first year of the crisis, but also reflects the winding down of private investment related to the Olympics.

The very disparate conditions across sectors is likely to have contributed to the recent high volatility of business investment data, which makes it hard to identify an underlying trend: for example, a very strong outcome in the March quarter of 1999 was followed by a decline in the June quarter. The latest Capital Expenditure Survey suggests that business investment is likely to have remained rather subdued lately, mainly on account of slowing mining investment offsetting much of the solid investment of manufacturing and services sectors. There is also the risk of some deferral of plant and equipment investment until after 1 July 2000, when the replacement of the old wholesale sales tax by GST will generally reduce the cost of investment.

The external side

In response to the crisis in East Asian economies and the associated weakening of world demand, growth of *merchandise export volumes* slowed down – on a seasonally adjusted basis – in the two quarters to March 1998 and has broadly stagnated since (Figure 7). Although this is in stark contrast to the average growth rates of 8 to 9 per cent recorded over the 1990-97 period, the stabilisation of export volumes in the face of sharply contracting demand in major markets is a remarkable performance which largely reflects the successful diversion of exports to more buoyant destinations elsewhere. This is particularly evident for resource exports, which are relatively homogeneous and can often be sold in alternative markets at prevailing world prices. Latest indicators suggest that export growth strengthened in the September quarter of 1999, which in part is a reflection of Asian economies recovering from the crisis.

Assisted by the depreciation of the Australian dollar, *services export volumes* also held up quite well in 1998-99 with tourism remaining buoyant despite a significant fall in visitors from East Asia; there were even signs of some pick-up of tourism from East Asia (excluding Japan) in the June quarter of 1999. Altogether, in the second half of 1998 real *exports of goods and services* recovered from their crisis-induced contraction and posted a small increase in FY 1998-99, in spite of the sharp fall in the March quarter of 1999. *Imports of goods and services* remained rather robust, but lost some of their momentum. This was probably a lagged effect of the strong import price increases (at the wholesale level) as a consequence of exchange rate depreciation. An important single factor which dampened the dynamism of imports was the levelling off from the middle of 1998 of the very strong domestic demand for motor vehicles, which was at the origin of soaring car imports. In consequence, the negative contribution of the real foreign balance to economic growth diminished, partly compensating for the effect of decelerating domestic demand on real GDP growth.

Current account

World commodity prices expressed in US dollars fell steeply during the two years after the onset of the Asian crisis in mid-1997, which implied a substantial deterioration in Australia's *terms of trade* (Figure 7, Panel C). However, export prices expressed in Australian dollars held up well during FY 1997-98 due to the marked exchange rate depreciation, which helped stabilise export values. But, the recovery of the Australian dollar *vis-à-vis* the US dollar since mid-1998 has led to a fall in export prices in local currency. Together with sluggish growth of export volumes, it resulted in sharply falling rural and resource export values, which

Figure 7. **Foreign trade indicators**

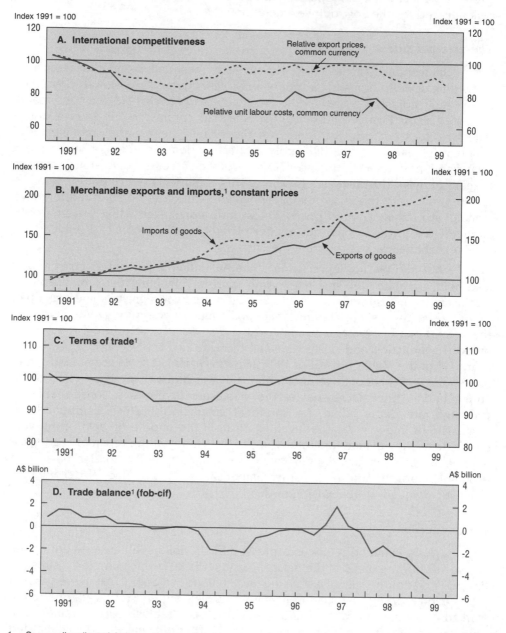

1. Seasonally adjusted; balance of payments basis.
Source: Australian Bureau of Statistics and OECD Secretariat.

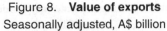

Figure 8. **Value of exports**
Seasonally adjusted, A$ billion

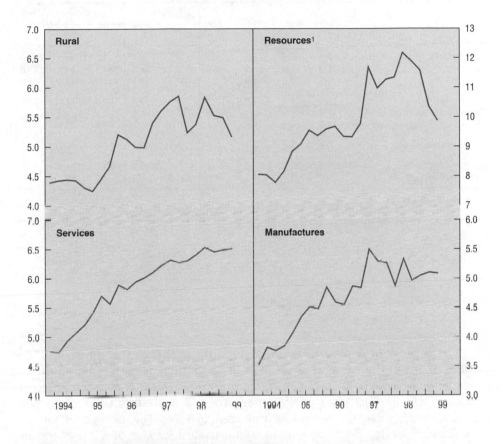

1. Includes non-rural commodity exports (including sugar) plus non-monetary gold.
Source: Reserve Bank of Australia and Australian Bureau of Statistics.

together account for around 60 per cent of goods and services exports in current prices (Figure 8). Altogether, the combination of a widening real trade deficit with deteriorating terms of trade led to a sharp negative swing in the *trade balance* (Figure 7, Panel D), from a surplus of A$ 2.3 billion[11] in the first half of 1997 to a deficit of A$ 8.7 billion (3 per cent of GDP) in the first half of 1999 but the worst of this deterioration may be past; first signs of recovering commodity prices became visible in the June quarter of 1999, when world base metal prices picked up again, which should help contain a further increase in the trade deficit.

Table 2. **Current account trends**[1]

A$ billion

	1995	1996	1997	1998	1997		1998		1999
					I	II	I	II	I
Trade balance	−5.6	−0.9	2.3	−8.3	2.3	0.0	−3.5	−4.8	−7.8
Exports	71.9	77.0	87.2	89.1	42.8	44.4	44.3	44.8	41.0
Imports	−77.5	−78.0	−84.9	−97.5	−40.5	−44.4	−47.9	−49.6	−48.9
Services, net	−20.4	−19.4	−19.3	−19.2	−9.5	−9.7	−9.5	−9.7	−10.0
Non-factor services, net	−1.2	0.0	−0.5	−1.8	0.0	−0.5	−0.7	−1.2	−0.9
Investment income, net	−19.2	−19.3	−18.8	−17.4	−9.6	−9.2	−8.8	−8.5	−9.1
Current transfers, net	−0.4	0.1	−0.3	−0.1	−0.2	−0.1	0.0	−0.1	0.2
Current balance	−26.4	−20.2	−17.2	−27.7	−7.4	−9.8	−13.0	−14.6	−17.6
As a percentage of GDP	−5.4	−3.9	−3.1	−4.8	−2.8	−3.5	−4.5	−5.0	−5.9

1. Seasonally adjusted.
Source: Australian Bureau of Statistics.

The *net services balance* remained broadly unchanged in 1998-99 as the growing deficit of the *non-factor services account* was largely offset by the improving *net investment income account* (Table 2). The latter improvement is mainly a reflection of falling debt interest rates on the large stock of Australia's net foreign debt – currently equivalent to around 38 per cent of GDP. The decline in interest payments on foreign debt more than compensated for the rise in net income payments from foreigners' direct ownership of Australian businesses. Contrary to past episodes of large swings in exchange rates, the lower external value of the Australian dollar during the Asian crisis had no significant effect on the net income deficit as over the past decade Australia's gross foreign-currency liabilities have become roughly equal to holdings of foreign-currency assets. Hence changes in debt-servicing costs in Australian dollars resulting from currency variations are roughly offset by a corresponding change in the return on foreign assets held by residents. This helped to contain the increase in the *current external deficit* to A$ 32.4 billion, 5.5 per cent of GDP, in FY 1998-99, following a deficit equivalent to 4 per cent in 1997-98. With a (seasonally adjusted) deficit equivalent to 6¼ per cent of GDP in the June quarter of 1999, there are so far no indications of a turnaround in the current external balance but this may be close to the cyclical peak.

The labour market

Employment growth gained momentum in 1998 and remained robust in the first ten months of 1999 (Table 3), recovering from a prolonged period of subdued labour market performance. The latter was a lagged effect of weaker economic activity in FY 1996-97. The key feature of the improving labour market was the resumption of the growth of full-time employment from late 1997, following little change during the preceding one-and-a-half years (Figure 9). Part-time employment remained buoyant; it continued to be boosted by the ongoing shift in the composition of production away from the secondary sector, where full-time employment dominates, to services, where the proportion of part-time jobs is much higher. As a consequence of the lagged response of employment to the

Table 3.   **The labour market**

Seasonally adjusted

	1995	1996	1997	1998	1998		1999		
					I	II	I	Q2	Q3
Civilian labour force[1]	2.6	1.3	1.0	1.5	1.2	1.8	1.2	1.1	1.2
Males	1.8	1.1	0.7	1.2	1.1	1.3	1.2	1.2	1.1
Females	3.6	1.6	1.3	1.8	1.2	2.4	1.3	1.0	1.2
Employed persons[1]	4.0	1.3	1.0	2.1	1.8	2.4	2.0	1.8	2.1
Full-time	3.3	1.0	0.0	1.8	1.6	2.0	1.3	1.2	1.5
Part-time	8.0	2.1	4.0	2.9	2.4	3.5	4.0	3.6	3.9
Unemployment rate[2]	8.5	8.5	8.5	8.0	8.1	7.9	7.4	7.4	7.2
Males	8.8	8.8	8.7	8.2	8.2	8.1	7.5	7.5	7.2
Females	8.1	8.2	8.3	7.7	7.9	7.6	7.3	7.3	7.1
Juniors looking for full-time work	27.7	27.9	27.7	27.6	27.9	27.4	23.7	23.5	22.0
Participation rate[2]	63.7	63.6	63.2	63.3	63.2	63.3	63.0	63.0	63.2
Males	73.9	73.7	73.1	72.9	72.9	72.9	72.7	72.7	72.7
Females	53.7	53.8	53.7	53.9	53.7	54.1	53.7	53.7	54.1
Overtime (hours)[2, 3, 5]	1.2	1.1	1.1	1.0	1.0	1.0	1.1	1.0	1.0
Average weekly hours worked[2, 4]									
Total	34.6	34.0	34.6	34.6	34.1	35.2	33.7	34.1	34.8
Full-time	40.9	40.3	41.1	41.3	40.5	42.0	40.2	40.9	41.5
Part-time	15.3	15.2	15.4	15.6	15.4	15.8	15.3	15.4	15.7
Job vacancies (thousand)[5]	57.3	60.8	64.5	74.8	77.4	72.8	71.6	77.4	83.4

1.   Percentage change from previous period at annual rates.
2.   Levels
3.   All industries, per employee.
4.   Not seasonally adjusted.
5.   Quarterly data based on mid-month of quarter.
Source: Australian Bureau of Statistics.

Figure 9.   **Patterns of employment**
Changes since January 1993

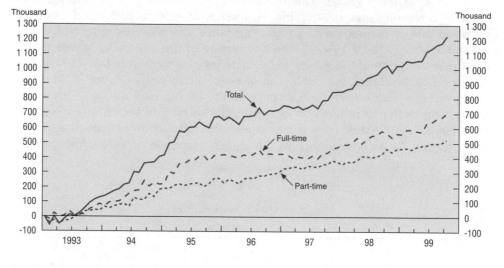

Source: Australian Bureau of Statistics.

Figure 10.   **Unemployment and vacancies**
Seasonally adjusted

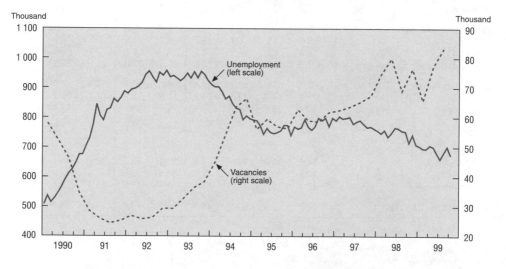

Source: Australian Bureau of Statistics.

re-acceleration of output growth, hourly labour productivity in the market sector[12] rose by $3^1/_2$ per cent in 1998 and by an annual rate of $3^1/_4$ per cent in the first half of 1999, hence above its trend rate of around 3 per cent since the beginning of the current expansion.

The recovery of employment since late 1997 was most pronounced in industries which benefited from the strength of domestic demand, such as construction, property and business services, health and community services, transport and storage, and retail trade, but also the public sector. Employment in construction has continued to grow, reflecting continued work on major Olympics-related projects and high levels of dwelling construction activity in the housing sector. Employment was generally weaker in those industries which were hit by sluggish foreign demand, for example manufacturing, mining and agriculture. Recent overall vacancy data of the Australian Bureau of Statistics (ABS) have been unusually volatile, which makes their interpretation difficult (Figure 10). However, vacancies for skilled workers were $8^1/_4$ per cent higher than a year earlier in October 1999. Together with robust growth of job advertisements, it is suggestive of a continuation of firm labour demand in the near term.

In contrast to earlier episodes of cyclical upswing, when strong growth in the economy tended to draw people into the labour force, both male and female labour force participation remained broadly unchanged during 1998 and even declined in the first half of 1999. With the female participation rate being roughly in line with major industrial countries, there is the possibility that its recent fall heralds some slowing of its long-term trend increase. Overall labour force participation may also have been contained by demographic factors, such as the ageing of the population and the movement of the "baby boomer" generation into lower participation cohorts. Moreover, it is conceivable that rising private wealth and lower mortgage interest rates have opened opportunities for some households to opt for more leisure and less work.

As a consequence of the stable and then falling labour force participation and its implied dampening effect on labour force growth, the recovery of employment was associated with a marked decline in unemployment; teenage and long-term unemployment have also declined. After staying broadly unchanged at a little above the 8 per cent mark for the three quarters ending in mid-1998, the unemployment rate fell quite rapidly thereafter to 7.2 per cent (seasonally-adjusted) in the September quarter of 1999 and to 7.1 per cent in October. This is close to earlier estimates of the non-accelerating inflation rate of unemployment (NAIRU) which many researchers had put in the $6^1/_2$ to $7^1/_2$ per cent range for the mid-1990s. However, the more recent study by Gruen, Pagan and Thompson (1999), which captures data affected by reforms of product and labour markets, arrives at estimates of the structural rate of unemployment of between $5^1/_2$ and 7 per cent at the end of their sample in 1997. This is largely in accordance with the latest estimate of the structural unemployment rate of 6½ per cent for the 1980s and 1990s derived from the Treasury Macroeconomic (TRYM) model.[13] Given that the benefits of recent structural reforms are likely to be still accruing, future estimates of the NAIRU could turn out even lower. Lower NAIRU estimates than hitherto are consistent with the observation that the recent marked decrease in the unemployment rate has not provoked any signs to date of accelerating wage or price inflation.

Price and wage inflation

Notwithstanding the robust economic growth and the potential inflation-ary consequences of the marked effective exchange rate depreciation until late 1998, inflation remained low (Figure 11). During twelve consecutive quarters end-ing in September 1999, consumer price inflation remained below 2 per cent, the lower boundary of the Reserve Bank's medium-term inflation target (see Chap-ter II below). Inflation had even been negative during the three quarters to March 1998, mainly owing to mortgage interest rate reductions.[14] In recent quarters, it has picked up somewhat to 1.7 per cent in the September quarter of 1999. Adjusting for the introduction of the government's 30 per cent private health insurance rebate, the CPI increase over the year to the September 1999 quarter was 2.1 per cent. Other measures of underlying inflation have also picked up slightly to around 2 per cent.

Contrary to most expectations, the steep depreciation of the Australian dollar in the context of the Asian crisis has had no visible adverse impact on "headline" inflation so far; prices of imported items in the CPI continued to fall, holding down the aggregate inflation rate rather than boosting it (Figure 12). The only noticeable effect of the lower exchange rate was a stabilisation of the (nega-tive) import price inflation at the consumer level in the range from –1 to –2 per cent over FY 1998-99, ending its earlier steep downward trend. Much of the fall in the price of imported items in the CPI owes to a 12½ per cent cut in the price of imported cars over the two fiscal years 1997-98 and 1998-99, mainly reflecting excess capacity of Asian car producers, falling tariff levels and the appreciation of the currency against the Korean Won. This induced a fall in overall car prices at the retail level by some 7 per cent over the past two years and reduced the underlying rate of inflation by about ½ percentage point each year. Measures of home-made goods prices and private sector service prices continued to rise at annual rates of around 2 per cent.

Over the past two years or so, prices of imported items recorded at the docks have moved broadly in line with fluctuations of the import-weighted effective exchange rate, without affecting prices at the retail level to any signifi-cant degree. Taken at face value, the lack of pass-through of price increases at the

Figure 11. **The achievement of low inflation**
Percentage change over four quarters

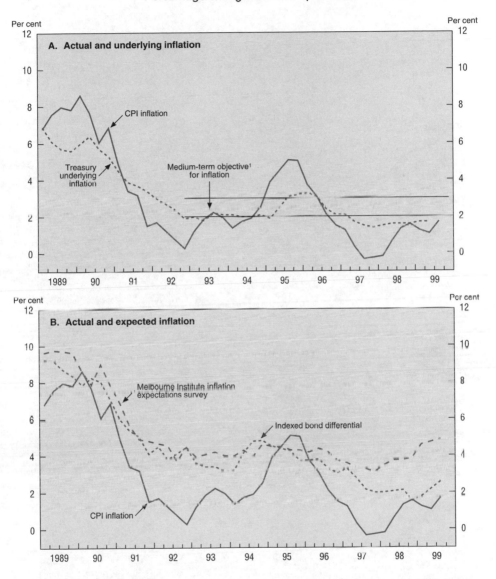

1. The inflation target was expressed in terms of underlying inflation up to late 1998. Following the move from an outlays to an acquisitions approach to measuring consumer prices, the inflation target is now expressed in terms of the new "headline" CPI.

Source: Reserve Bank of Australia; University of Melbourne, Institute of Applied Economic and Social Research and OECD, *Main Economic Indicators.*

Figure 12.   **Selected components of inflation**
Year-on-year change

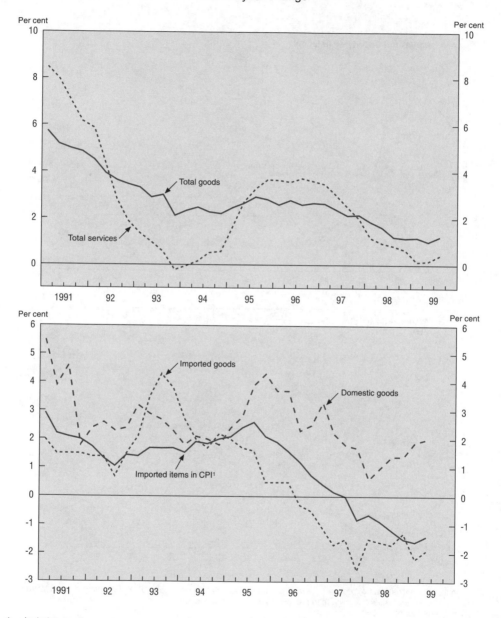

1.   Includes services.
Source: Reserve Bank of Australia and OECD, *Main Economic Indicators.*

docks to consumers from mid-1997 to late 1998 suggests that importers' or retailers' margins have been heavily squeezed and that previously observed lags in the transmission of import price rises seem no longer to apply. Although this may be explained as the consequence of tougher competition in domestic markets, it is somewhat puzzling in the face of prevailing strong demand. Apart from recording problems, a possible explanation would be that increased use of exchange-rate hedging operations may have given importers greater insulation from exchange-rate movements than in the past. The strengthening of the Australian dollar, both in trade-weighted as well as in import-weighted terms, since early 1999 no doubt helped the importers to restore much of their profit margins. This may prevent the earlier depreciation-induced import price increases at the dock level ever being passed on to consumers to any great extent.

Recent indicators of inflation expectations depict a rather disparate picture across different groups of the population. The Melbourne Institute survey of consumers' inflation expectations for the coming year – the only available information of household inflation expectations – indicates a strong increase since the beginning of 1999, to around 5 per cent in recent months (Figure 11, Panel B). However, although tracking movements quite well, this indicator has generally overstated the level of actual inflation by a large margin. Business surveys continue to indicate that firms are planning only moderate price increases in the near term, although latest surveys confirm that the downward trend in business price expectations has now halted. A survey[15] of trade union officials is for expected inflation of 3¼ per cent by mid-2000. Implicit in the yield difference between 10-year bonds and indexed bonds of the same maturity, financial market participants appear to have raised their inflation forecast for the next twelve months by 1 percentage point since early 1999 to 2¾ per cent in the September quarter of 1999. Given that the horizon of this implicit projection covers the introduction of GST in July 2000, it is likely that this measure of inflation expectations makes allowance for the GST effect on consumer prices.

Low inflation outcomes were underpinned by moderate wage growth. Combined with the strong labour productivity gains noted above, this resulted in only mild increases in unit labour costs (Table 4). The new Wage Cost Index[16] (WCI) recorded an average increase in wage rates (excluding bonuses) of 3.2 per cent in FY 1998-99, the first full year for which a wage rate in this definition is available. In the same period, average weekly ordinary-time earnings of adults working full-time (AWOTE) grew by 3.7 per cent, with some deceleration to 3.2 per cent in the first half of 1999. The growth in AWOTE during the four quarters to the September 1999 quarter even fell to 2.3 per cent, the lowest rate recorded in more than six years. Both WCI and AWOTE suggest wage growth to have been stronger in the public than in the private sector. Given that the WCI is constructed as an indicator of wages for a basket of constant-quality jobs, above-average

Table 4. **Costs and prices**

Percentage change from corresponding period of previous year

	1995	1996	1997	1998	1997-98[1]	1998-99[1]	1998 Q3	1998 Q4	1999 Q1	1999 Q2	1999 Q3
National accounts deflators											
Private consumption	1.9	1.7	1.4	1.3	1.4	1.2	1.4	1.3	1.2	1.1	1.1
Total domestic demand	0.9	1.2	1.2	1.1	1.2	1.4	1.6	1.4	1.5	1.2	1.2
GDP	1.5	2.0	1.4	0.3	1.2	0.4	0.3	-0.1	0.9	0.7	0.7
Exports of goods and services	5.9	-2.6	-0.1	2.3	4.3	-3.6	3.6	-3.9	-4.8	-9.0	
Imports of goods and services	3.2	-6.5	-1.5	6.9	4.3	1.6	9.8	3.7	-1.1	-5.4	
Consumer price index	4.6	2.6	0.3	0.9	0.0	1.2	1.3	1.6	1.2	1.1	1.7
Underlying inflation	2.7	2.7	1.7	1.6	1.5	1.7	1.6	1.6	1.7	1.7	:
Wage cost index (excluding bonuses)											
Total	:	:	:	:	:	3.2	3.3	3.1	3.0	3.2	
Private sector	:	:	:	:	:	3.0	3.2	3.0	2.8	2.9	
Public sector	:	:	:	:	:	3.8	3.7	3.6	4.1	3.9	
Average weekly earnings											
All employees	2.8	3.0	3.1	2.8	3.2	2.4	3.5	1.9	1.8	2.5	0.4
Ordinary time, full-time work (AWOTE)	4.8	3.9	4.0	4.2	4.1	3.7	4.1	4.2	3.1	3.3	2.1
Private sector, ordinary time, full-time work (AWOTE)	5.9	3.9	3.5	4.0	4.0	3.4	4.1	3.7	2.6	3.2	1.8
Public sector, ordinary time, full-time work (AWOTE)	3.2	4.9	6.1	5.0	4.8	5.1	4.7	6.0	5.2	4.7	3.8
Nominal non-farm unit labour costs[2]	2.7	2.5	1.2	0.5	0.1	1.3	0.6	1.4	0.8	2.5	

1. Fiscal year begins 1 July.
2. Seasonally-adjusted series derived by the Treasury.
Source: Australian Bureau of Statistics, Commonwealth Treasury and Reserve Bank of Australia.

government sector wage increases may partly reflect factors other than compositional changes in the structure of employment.

Latest federal enterprise agreements, which cover around one-fifth of all employees, confirm the moderating trend of wages. Moreover, in its Safety Net Review of April 1999, the Australian Industrial Relations Commission (AIRC) conceded weekly award rate adjustments which translate into wage increases for representative job classifications of 2 to 3 per cent. At the same time, the federal minimum wage was raised by 3.2 per cent, following an increase of 3.9 per cent in 1998. It is estimated that the decision of the AIRC will contribute ⅓ percentage point to the growth in AWOTE this year, after ½ percentage point in 1998.

The outlook to 2001

Overview of the present situation

Economic activity remains buoyant, mainly reflecting strong growth in consumer expenditure. Household wealth has been rising rapidly, mainly on account of capital gains on houses and, to a lesser extent, on shares. This has encouraged households to borrow to expand consumption expenditures more rapidly than disposable incomes. On the other hand, growth in investment expenditure is slowing, mainly reflecting falling mining investment. Prices for the commodities that Australia exports remain weak and, in Australian dollar terms, have fallen sharply this year. The prices for imported goods and services in the CPI continue to decline, mainly reflecting falling prices for motor vehicles. Despite strong employment growth and a significant decline in unemployment in the past year, wage pressures remain subdued.

Current economic indicators generally point to some slowing in economic activity in coming months. The trend monthly growth rate in retail sales has slowed from the very high rates reached at the beginning of the year. The passing of the one-off boost to consumer expenditure provided by the AMP demutualisation and by the large capital gains from the first stage of the Telstra float also suggest that growth in consumer expenditure might weaken in coming months. In addition, consumers may delay purchasing major household items and motor vehicles, as indirect tax on these items will decline once the tax package is implemented in July 2000. On the other hand, consumer confidence remains very high, suggesting that any slowing in consumer expenditure is likely to be moderate. Building approvals for private dwellings have been rising in trend terms in recent months and growth in personal housing credit has picked up, suggesting that housing activity may strengthen in coming months.

The June quarter capital expenditure (CAPEX) survey shows that businesses expect to reduce nominal investment by 8 per cent in FY 1999-2000, based on the average difference between outcomes and plans over the last five years. This mainly reflects a 30 per cent decline in mining investment. Investment in other sectors is expected to be fairly flat, despite high corporate profitability and business confidence. Low commodity prices are weighing on investment intentions in resource-related manufacturing while many other manufacturers are subject to strong competition from Asian producers. In addition, investment related to the Sydney Olympics is falling. Even so, the upwards revision in expectations in the June quarter CAPEX survey from the previous survey, together with a generally favourable environment for investment (high profits, low interest rates and readily available finance) point to a somewhat smaller decline in investment expenditure than indicated in the survey. Inventories increased markedly in the first half of 1999, continuing the strong growth apparent since the March quarter 1998, correcting the previous large rundown in stocks. Desired stock levels appear to have increased as the growth in domestic demand has proved to be stronger than had generally been expected by businesses. Job vacancy series continue to grow strongly, pointing to further high growth in employment.

Current projections and underlying assumptions[17]

With growth expected to remain relatively strong and with inflation expected to rise, the monetary authorities are assumed to raise short-term official interest rates by a further 0.75 percentage point in 2000. Fiscal policy settings are based on those outlined in the FY 1999-2000 budgets for the Commonwealth and the States and Territories, adjusted for the tax package as passed into law (see Chapters II and III below). On this basis, the general government budget balance is projected by the OECD Secretariat to remain in surplus and to oscillate in a narrow range between $\frac{1}{2}$ and $\frac{3}{4}$ per cent of GDP through to 2001. The other main assumptions underlying the projections are that:

- the average price of internationally traded oil is US$21 in the second half of 1999 and constant in real terms thereafter;
- prices (expressed in SDRs) for Australia's non-oil commodity exports rise over the projection period, resulting in increases in the terms of trade of $2\frac{1}{2}$ per cent in 2000 and 1 per cent in the following year;
- growth in Australia's export markets for goods rises sharply in 1999, to $7\frac{1}{2}$ per cent, and only eases slightly in the following two years;
- nominal exchange rates remain unchanged from their levels of 25 October, implying that, on average, the effective exchange rate is broadly stable in 1999 and subsequent years but that the Australian dollar appreciates against the US dollar by 3 per cent in 1999 and is broadly unchanged thereafter.

On these assumptions, output growth is projected to slow, from 5 per cent in 1998 to 4 per cent in 1999, mainly reflecting a reduced rate of stock building

Table 5.   **Short-term prospects**

Percentage changes

	Percentage share of GDP in 1996 at current prices	1997	1998	1999	2000	2001
A. Demand and output at constant 1997-98 prices						
Private consumption	58.9	3.9	4.3	4.8	3.8	3.5
Public consumption	18.6	1.9	2.7	4.2	2.2	2.3
Gross fixed capital formation	22.3	11.4	6.1	3.4	1.6	3.7
of which:						
Government	2.3	7.7	2.2	2.1	0.5	2.4
Private[1]	20.0	12.1	6.4	3.6	1.8	3.8
Dwellings[2]	4.4	14.4	12.6	3.7	2.6	1.0
Other building and structures	3.3	8.8	26.4	−11.7	−6.0	−3.0
Machine and equipment and intangible fixed assets	8.8	17.1	2.1	5.4	3.0	7.0
Public enterprises	2.1	−6.6	−21.3	37.2	5.0	5.0
Final domestic demand	99.9	5.2	4.4	4.4	3.0	3.3
Increase in stocks[3]	0.3	−1.6	1.7	0.5	−0.4	0.0
Total domestic demand	100.2	3.6	6.2	4.8	2.5	3.3
Exports of goods and services	19.3	11.5	−0.4	2.8	7.8	7.6
Imports of goods and services	19.5	10.3	5.9	6.5	4.0	5.6
Change in foreign balance[3]	−0.2	0.2	−1.3	−0.8	0.7	0.3
Statistical discrepancy	0.0	0.0	0.2	−0.2	−0.3	0.3
GDP	100.0	3.9	5.1	3.9	3.0	4.0
B. Other Items						
Private consumption deflator		1.4	1.3	1.4	4.2	3.5
Employment (LFS definition)		1.0	2.1	1.9	1.7	1.9
Unemployment rate (per cent)		8.5	8.0	7.3	6.9	6.5
General government financial balance		−0.6	0.3	0.7	0.5	0.6
Current balance (A$ billion)		−17.1	−28.0	−34.9	−31.7	−29.6
Current balance (per cent of GDP)		−3.1	−4.8	−5.7	−4.9	−4.3

1.   Including public trading enterprises.
2.   Including real estate transfer expenses.
3.   Contribution to changes in real GDP (as a percentage of real GDP in the previous period).
Source: OECD Secretariat.

and slowing fixed investment (Table 5). Falling investment in the mining sector is expected to underpin a further decline in the growth rate of fixed investment in 2000, contributing to another reduction in output growth, to 3 per cent. However the main factor underlying this weakening in growth is consumption expenditure, which is projected to grow more slowly as the one-off effects that boosted growth in late 1998 and early 1999 pass and as capital gains on housing and shares decline. Output growth is projected to pick up to 4 per cent in 2001 as business investment recovers. The strengthening international economic outlook, especially in Australia's major export markets, underpins an increase in export volume growth and in the terms of trade. Mainly as a result of these factors, the external current account deficit is projected to decline from 5¾ per cent of GDP in 1999 to 4¼ per cent in 2001.

Employment growth is projected to ease from almost 2 per cent in 1999 to around 1¾ per cent in 2000 on the back of the slowdown in economic activity but to rise again in the following year as activity strengthens. Such rates of employment growth should cut the (year-average) unemployment rate from a little over 7 per cent in 1999 to around 6½ per cent in 2001. Recent increases in oil prices and the improving international economy are likely to result in firmer prices for imported goods and services in the CPI. This, together with a small rise in wage increases should push up the underlying inflation rate from around 1¾ per cent in 1999 to about 2½ per cent in 2001. The introduction of the tax package in July 2000 is assumed to add 2¾ percentage points to the price level in the year after its introduction but somewhat less in subsequent years when some State indirect taxes are abolished and as full access to input credits on motor vehicles purchased by businesses are phased in.

There are major sources of risk on both the domestic and international fronts. On the external side, the US economy could slow more than is assumed if there were to be a sharp correction in its financial markets. Such a development could also have adverse effects on the nascent recovery in Asia. Moreover, should Asian countries fail to complete the structural reforms that are necessary to improve the functioning of their capital markets, the recent burst of growth could prove to be short-lived. Such developments would adversely affect Australia's exports and growth prospects as well as delaying improvement in the current account balance. Domestically, there is the risk that demand may not slow significantly, raising concerns about inflation pressures. This could occur if house prices continue their rapid increase, encouraging households to go on borrowing to finance growth in consumer expenditures in excess of disposable income. Finally, the introduction of the GST could raise underlying inflation expectations owing to the difficulty of distinguishing GST-related price increases from underlying inflation. While consumers will be fully compensated for the one-off effects of the GST on prices, these developments will need to be carefully watched if the current expansion in activity is to be sustained.

II. Macroeconomic policies

Sound macroeconomic policies have contributed substantially to Australia's impressive economic performance in recent years, as evidenced in particular by the economy's ability to weather the adverse international conditions since the financial crisis in East Asia became apparent in July 1997. The key to this good performance on the macroeconomic front has been the setting of both monetary and fiscal policy in a medium-term framework over a number of years. This has given a degree of macroeconomic stability which, together with the structural reforms discussed in the next chapter, has provided the right climate for sustained growth.

Monetary policy, which operates in a medium-term inflation targeting[18] framework, based on central bank independence and a floating exchange rate regime, has delivered low inflation since 1992. The operational objective of the Reserve Bank (RBA) is to maintain the rate of inflation[19] on average at around 2 to 3 per cent over the course of the business cycle while keeping monetary conditions conducive to sustainable growth in output and employment. Although consistent with the RBA's flexible approach to inflation targeting, the fall in the underlying rate of inflation to slightly below its lower target bound opened up room for five consecutive cuts in the target cash rate from July 1996 to July 1997. Persistently low inflation also allowed the Reserve Bank to tolerate the substantial depreciation of the exchange rate and the implied easing of monetary conditions, which accompanied the financial market turmoil until late 1998.

Fiscal policy, which has been aimed at a balanced budget on average over the economic cycle, moved the Commonwealth finances from deficit into balance[20] in 1997-98 and into surplus in 1998-99, with prospects of further improvements in government finances in the years ahead. This contributed to a high degree of confidence among consumers and investors, which supported economic growth and falling unemployment in spite of the negative impact of the Asian economic crisis. The following paragraphs review monetary and fiscal policy developments since the middle of 1998 in more detail. The Chapter also tries to give a rough estimate of the contribution of sound macroeconomic policies to the economy's growth performance in the face of the Asian crisis.

Monetary management

Interest rate developments

Although the Reserve Bank left policy interest rates unchanged during the $1\frac{1}{2}$ years following the cut in the target cash rate[21] from 5.5 to 5 per cent in July 1997, a number of lending rates tended to come down further during 1998 as intensified competition continued to compress the interest margins of financial intermediaries. This was most pronounced for banks' variable-rate loans to small businesses, which fell by more than 100 basis points from January to November 1998, to around $7\frac{3}{4}$ per cent. In addition, monetary conditions had eased as a consequence of exchange rate depreciation. Nevertheless, in December 1998, the RBA decided to cut the target cash rate by another 25 basis points to 4.75 per cent (Table 6). This brought the cash rate down to its previous cyclical low of 1993-94 and to the level which the US Federal fund rate had adopted since November 1998. The decision was based on the anticipation of a significant slowdown in world growth in 1999, its expected negative implications for Australia's economic growth and the assessment that inflation was well under control, in spite of the decline in the exchange rate during the preceding eighteen months.

Money market interest rates rapidly followed the December 1998 cash rate cut, in accordance with market expectations of unchanged monetary policy in the foreseeable future (Figure 13). However, when expectations about an interest rate hike by the US Federal Reserve built up in the course of the first half of 1999, markets anticipated the RBA to follow the imminent US Federal Reserve tightening. In consequence, the interest rate for three-month bank bills detached from the cash rate, rising to close to 5 per cent by late June, where it remained for some months before rising to around 5.4 per cent on markets' expectations of a tightening by the Reserve Bank, and as Y2K factors distorted slightly the short-term yield curve. With the increase in the cash rate to 5 per cent on 3 November 1999, the three month bank bill rate remained virtually unchanged as the move had been widely anticipated in the markets.

Lending rates have also responded to changes in the cash rate. The cash rate cut of December 1998 induced another round of interest rate reductions across a broad variety of variable-rate business and housing loans in late 1998 and early 1999, on average in line with the cut in the cash rate. The adjustment of lending rates to the new cash rate level combined with squeezed interest margins as a result of enhanced competition induced financial intermediates' lending rates to fall substantially below the previous cyclical lows of 1993-94 (Figure 14). After their alignment to the new cash rate level had been concluded, lending rates in general remained unchanged until mid-1999. Lending rates on some categories of banks' fixed-rate housing and business loans, which are usually

Table 6.   **Changes in official interest rates 1994-99**

	Change	New cash rate target
	Percentage points	Per cent
A. Tightening		
17 August 1994	+ 0.75	5.50
24 October 1994	+ 1.00	6.50
14 December 1994	+ 1.00	7.50
B. Easing		
31 July 1996	−0.50	7.00
6 November 1996	−0.50	6.50
11 December 1996	−0.50	6.00
23 May 1997	−0.50	5.50
30 July 1997	−0.50	5.00
2 December 1998	−0.25	4.75
C. Tightening		
3 November 1999	+0.25	5.00

Source: Reserve Bank of Australia, *Bulletin*, various issues.

Figure 13.   **Money and capital market interest rates**

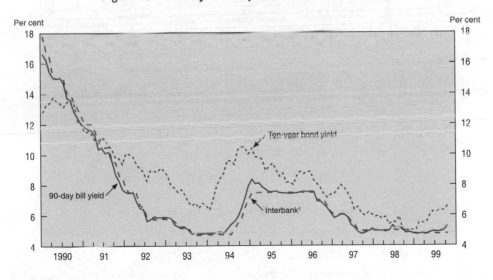

1.   Cash market, 11 a.m. call rate.
Source: Reserve Bank of Australia.

Figure 14. **Lending rates**

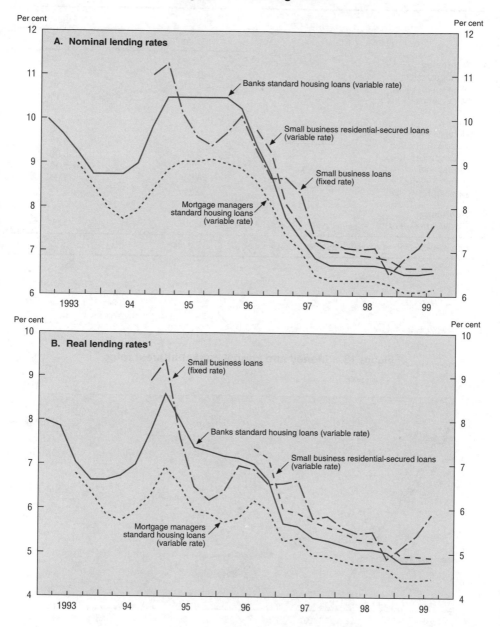

1. Nominal rates less the Treasury underlying rate inflation until the June quarter of 1999 (less CPI inflation thereafter).
Source: Reserve Bank of Australia and Australian Bureau of Statistics.

funded in the capital market, edged up by ½ and 1 percentage point in the September quarter, respectively, in response to higher capital market interest rates (see below); the tightening of certain lending rates probably also reflects the strong demand for credit. Following the ¼ percentage point increase in the cash rate in November 1999, most of the major banks have increased their standard variable home loan rates by the same amount. Given the recent increase in measures of expected inflation as well as the minor increase in underlying inflation, various indicators of *real* lending rates have continued to fall during 1998 and in 1999, to their lowest levels since the first half of the 1980s.

Ten-year Treasury bonds bottomed out at around 4¾ per cent in October 1998, the lowest rate since 1965. This was largely a reflection of low actual and expected inflation as well as the global fall in high-quality bond yields as a result of the flight into government bonds issued by highly rated countries. When the global outlook improved and fears of inflation pressures emerged, Australian bond yields picked up in early 1999, in parallel with US bond rates (Figure 15). Bond yields rose to 6¾ per cent in October 1999, some 1¾ percentage point above their trough of the second half of 1998, but still rather low by historical standards as well as in comparison with the level prevailing as recently as the mid-1990s. The latest rise in nominal bond yields outpaced the increase in proxies of inflation expectations so that estimates of real bond yields have picked up in 1999, albeit from a very low level and still considerably below their previous cyclical trough in 1993-94 (Figure 16). The broadly simultaneous rise of global bond yields left the Australia-United States ten-year bond rate differential at around the low level it had achieved in the course of 1997, in the range of 20 to 40 basis points, although this spread widened to about 60 basis points in late October. The persistently low spread is in stark contrast to the differential of over 250 basis points observed in mid-1995. It bears witness to the improved perception of Australia's credit standing, influenced no doubt by the sustained improvement in the government finances and by several years of low inflation.

Financial intermediation

Low nominal and real cost of credit were conducive to vigorous growth of financial intermediaries' lending to the private non-financial sector: it increased at an annual rate of about 11 per cent during the year ending in mid-1999 (Table 7); this more than reversed the brief slowdown in credit expansion seen in mid-1998. Within the total, credit to households continued to grow rapidly, consistent with the strength of consumption expenditures. While progressive use of credit cards has contributed to this growth, a large part of it is also due to the increased availability of residentially-secured lines of credit to households in recent years, which carry a lower interest charge than unsecured personal lending. In line with slowing investment, business credit growth decelerated somewhat during the

Figure 15. **International comparison of long-term interest rates**

Ten-year bond yield

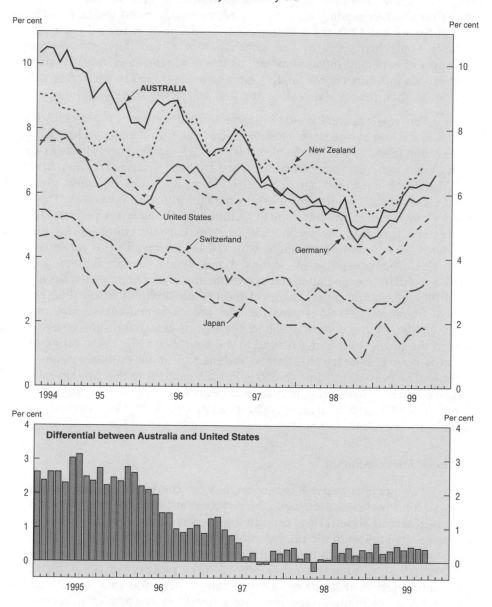

Source: OECD, *Main Economic Indicators* and *Economic Outlook*.

Figure 16. **Real asset yields**

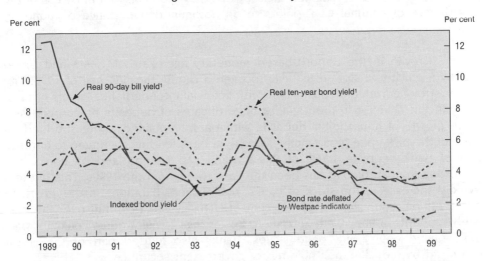

1. Nominal rates less the Treasury underlying rate inflation until the June quarter of 1999 (less CPI inflation thereafter).
Source: Reserve Bank of Australia; University of Melbourne, Institute of Applied Economic and Social Research and
OECD, *Main Economic Indicators.*

Table 7. **Financial aggregates**[1]

Seasonally adjusted annualised growth rates, per cent

	Six months to:		Three months to:	
	December 1998	June 1999	March 1999	June 1999
Total credit	10.5	11.3	12.2	10.5
Personal	17.2	14.9	18.6	11.4
Housing	11.0	14.0	13.8	14.2
Business	8.2	8.5	9.6	7.5
Currency	9.5	7.9	7.8	8.0
M1	1.3	12.5	17.0	8.2
M3	6.3	14.0	11.9	16.1
Broad money	7.8	12.0	9.0	15.1

1. Adjusted for major breaks in series.
Source: Reserve Bank of Australia.

June quarter of 1999. Altogether, the rapid credit expansion well in excess of the growth rate of nominal GDP points to an accommodative stance of monetary policy.

Growth in the deposit-based monetary aggregates M1, M3 and broad money[22] which had slowed in 1998, recovered during the first half of 1999. The recent strong growth of deposits held with financial intermediaries largely owes to a significant increase in the issuance of certificates of deposits by corporations, while growth of households' deposits with banks remained rather subdued. In spite of the pick-up in broad money, growth of bank lending continued to outpace that of bank deposits. Much of this funding gap was bridged by banks' net borrowing from abroad, as has been the case throughout the 1990s. This led to a fivefold increase in the stock of banks' net offshore liabilities in the 1990s, to A\$ 75 billion, equivalent to 13 per cent of GDP, in late 1998. But over the past twelve months or so, growth in offshore borrowings has slowed as banks increasingly raised equity and bond issues. Banks also funded part of the credit extended by reducing their holdings of government securities.

Exchange rate behaviour

Since the onset of the Asian crisis in July 1997, Australian financial markets have been heavily affected by global developments. In particular, Australia's strong trade links with the troubled region and the adverse effect of the crisis on world commodity prices induced international investors to reduce their Australian dollar holdings, which caused the dollar to depreciate substantially. The Australian dollar also came under some bouts of intensive speculative selling pressure, to which the RBA responded by temporary interventions in the foreign exchange market. But in contrast to other central banks experiencing similar pressures, the RBA considered an increase in policy interest rates as inappropriate as the inflation target was not in jeopardy: although the depreciation in the exchange rate was expected to lead to some increase in inflation, a persistent overshooting of the target was deemed unlikely. Moreover, the selling pressures on the Australian dollar were not judged to be based on any loss of confidence in policy setting in Australia. In consequence, the Reserve Bank accepted the Australian dollar's loss of nearly one-quarter of its value against the US dollar from July 1997 through to the September quarter of 1998 (Figure 17). But given its marked appreciation against troubled Asian countries, the Australian dollar depreciated in standard trade-weighted terms[23] by a relatively small 11½ per cent over the same period. And if adjusted for differential movements in consumer prices (unit labour costs), the real effective exchange rate of the Australian dollar fell by some 11 (16) per cent from the outbreak of the Asian crisis until late 1998. Hence, in addition to low

Figure 17. **Exchange rates**

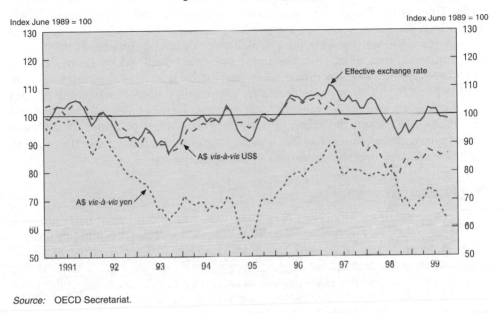

Index June 1989 = 100

Index June 1989 = 100

Source: OECD Secretariat.

nominal and real interest rates, the Australian dollar's depreciation in the context of the Asian crisis contributed heavily to the easing of an overall monetary conditions.

The Australian dollar's exchange rate *vis-à-vis* the US dollar bottomed out in the September quarter of 1998 and has trended up since, helped by growing evidence of solid growth of the Australian economy in spite of the Asian financial crisis, and clear indications of persistent low inflation. The exchange rate was further supported in the first half of 1999 when some commodity prices showed first signs of recovery, in part reflecting the gradual improvement in market sentiment about the world economic outlook. In addition, prices of base metals responded positively to cuts in production and mine closures. However, with the ongoing strength of the yen *vis-à-vis* the Australian dollar, the (trade-weighted) effective exchange rate turned around only in early 1999, gaining more than 9 per cent since then until July. In consequence, the CPI-based (unit-labour-cost based) real effective exchange rate appreciated by some 7 (9) per cent from late 1998 to mid-1999, exerting a tightening effect on overall monetary conditions. Since August 1999, however, the effective Australian dollar exchange rate has again lost some ground, weakening both against the US dollar and the yen.

The fall in commodity prices induced by the Asian crisis, which to a large extent was the driving force of the effective exchange rate depreciation of the

Australian dollar until the end of 1998, implied a deterioration in the terms of trade. This terms-of-trade loss has exerted a contractionary effect on the economy, which has partly offset the supportive effect of the exchange rate depreciation on economic activity: from their peak in the September quarter of 1997 to the low in the final quarter of 1998, the terms of trade[24] declined by 7½ per cent. A small recovery has been recorded since, so that by mid-1999 the terms-of-trade deterioration from the onset of the Asian crisis until mid-1999 was some 6½ per cent. Compared with earlier episodes, for example between September 1984 and December 1986, when the terms-of-trade loss amounted to about 17 per cent – the current deterioration has been more moderate, reflecting the decrease in the price of many imports expressed in foreign currency.

Overall monetary conditions

The divergent influences of real interest rates, the terms of trade and real exchanges rate can be summarised by a simple Monetary Conditions Index[25] (MCI). It suggests that in general, monetary conditions eased after the extent of the Asian crisis became apparent: the representative real short-term interest rate drifted downward and the real effective depreciation of the Australian dollar more than compensated for the contractionary effect of the terms-of-trade loss on the economy (Figure 18). Lately, the MCI has turned in the direction of rather neutral monetary conditions with the real exchange rate appreciating slightly and the terms of trade deteriorating somewhat, while the real three-month bill rate remained broadly unchanged. However, various indicators of the real cost of credit have continued to decline during the first half of 1999 (see Figure 14, Panel B), which is not reflected in the flat real short-term bill yield. Hence, current monetary conditions may be somewhat easier than suggested by a standard MCI.

The contribution of macroeconomic polices to sustaining growth during the Asian crisis

The rapid growth of the economy at the time when the Asian meltdown began and the inevitable decline in exports to the countries hit by the crisis implied that Australia's current account deficit was bound to widen. In addition, the crisis-induced depreciation of the Australian dollar engendered expectations of higher consumer price inflation as a consequence of rising import prices. In the face of these developments, monetary policy might have been tightened to counter these adverse effects of the Asian crisis, at the cost of lower output and employment, an option which had been subject to debate at the time. However, with underlying inflation below the medium-term inflation target band and expectations of an imminent slowing of output growth, the Reserve Bank opted in favour of an accommodating policy stance, leaving the cash rate unchanged through most of 1998, with a further quarter of percentage point reduction in

Figure 18. **Monetary conditions**

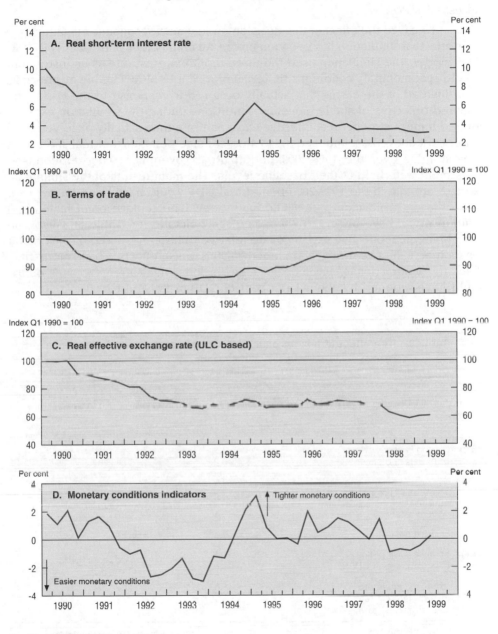

1. For technical details, see note 25.
Source: OECD Secretariat.

December 1998, and accepting the substantial depreciation in the exchange rate discussed above.

To gauge the effect of this decision on key macroeconomic magnitudes, a counterfactual simulation has been run on the Australia block of the OECD INTER-LINK model. The simulation used the three-month interest rate as an instrument to hold real monetary conditions (in terms of a simple MCI[26]) stable at pre-crisis level, instead of the easing that actually occurred in response to the crisis. The assumed objective of stable monetary conditions during the simulation exercise implied a much stronger real effective exchange rate than actually observed (8 to 11 per cent above baseline) and 3½ to 4 percentage points higher real short-term interest rates over the 1998-2000 period. Real government consumption and investment were held at their baseline levels. The main results of the simulation exercise are that in the 1999-2000 period real GDP would have been 1½ per cent lower, the unemployment rate would have been 1 percentage point higher and inflation would have been 2 to 2½ percentage points lower (Table 8). Given the much higher real effective exchange rate relative to baseline, and the consequent substantial export-reducing and import-raising price effects which more than offset the contractionary income effect on imports, the current account deficit would have widened by about 1 per cent of GDP in 1999 and 2000.

Table 8. **The effect of non-accommodating[1] monetary policy in response to the Asian crisis**

Differences from baseline in per cent

	1998	1999	2000
Total domestic demand (real)	−0.2	−0.5	−0.4
Real foreign balance	−0.6	−1.1	−1.0
Exports (goods and services)	−2.3	−4.5	−4.7
Imports (goods and services)	−0.9	1.1	0.4
GDP (real)	−0.9	−1.6	−1.5
Total unemployment	0.5	1.1	1.2
Unemployment rate[2]	0.5	1.0	1.1
Consumer price inflation[2]	−0.8	−1.9	−2.6
Current balance (US$ billion)	−3.7	−6.5	−6.0
Current balance (as % of GDP)[2]	−0.6	−1.1	−1.1
Real effective exchange rate	8.8	11.2	7.9
Real short term interest rate	3.5	3.8	3.8
Real long term interest rate	1.7	2.9	3.6

1. Unchanged monetary conditions, using short-term interest rate as instrument, as described in the text.
2. Change in level.
Source: OECD Interlink model.

In addition to accommodating monetary policy, fiscal consolidation since 1996-97 is likely to also have fostered the economy's robust performance in the face of the Asian crisis. Assuming that the private sector is unlikely to have reduced its savings so as to completely offset the rise in government savings, fiscal retrenchment has contributed to a lower underlying current external deficit. This means that when the Asian crisis hit, the current account deficit rose from a lower starting position. The lower actual current external deficit induced by fiscal consolidation is very likely to have enhanced the confidence of financial market participants in the stability of the Australian economy.

Another channel from fiscal rectitude to macroeconomic performance is that reduced indebtedness of the government (relative to GDP) is likely to have reduced the risk premium on Australian debt, thus contributing to lower capital market interest rates. Although it is difficult to explicitly spell out such effects in the framework of a macroeconomic model, it seems not unreasonable to assume that improved confidence in financial markets may have cut the general level of interest rates by around 1 percentage point. In view of the substantial decline in the Australia-United States bond yield differential observed since the mid-1990s, this might even appear to be a rather conservative assumption. According to the OECD INTERLINK model run in a flexible exchange rate mode, such a reduction in the general interest rate level would generate a level of real GDP 1 per cent higher and a current external deficit ½ per cent of GDP lower than would have otherwise been the case in 1999-2000 (Table 9). Hence, as the combined effect of

Table 9. **The impact of a one percentage point fall in nominal interest rates under floating exchange rates**

Differences from baseline in per cent

Variable	1998	1999	2000
Private consumption (real)	0.2	0.2	0.2
Final domestic demand (real)	0.2	0.3	0.4
Real foreign balance	0.4	0.5	0.6
GDP (real)	0.6	0.9	1.0
Total unemployment	−0.3	−0.5	−0.6
Unemployment rate[1]	−0.2	−0.4	−0.5
Consumer price inflation[1]	0.5	0.9	1.3
Current balance (US$ billion)	−2.1	−3.2	−3.8
Current balance (as % of GDP)[1]	−0.4	−0.6	−0.7
Real effective exchange rate	−4.4	−5.4	−5.8

1. Change in level.
Source: OECD Interlink model.

well-judged monetary and fiscal policy settings, real GDP may have been at least 2 per cent higher and the current external deficit some 1½ per cent of GDP lower in 1999-2000 than would have been the case if policies had not been adjusted.

The challenge of monetary policy ahead

In sum, monetary policy has been very successful in keeping inflation under control while at the same time restricting the negative impact of the Asian crisis on the domestic economy to a minimum. There are, however, challenges ahead, which will require continued vigilance of the Reserve Bank. The major challenge will be to deal with a significant shift in economic circumstances as the Asian crisis recedes and the economy enters a period of stronger growth prospects, with correspondingly greater risks to the inflation outlook. Whereas a significant economic slowdown in Australia had initially been expected to stem from the Asian crisis, it now appears likely that any slowing in growth will be relatively mild and of short duration. As the increase in the cash rate in November 1999 indicated, the generally stronger economic outlook suggested to the authorities that the expansionary setting of monetary policy that was maintained through the Asian crisis period was not fully appropriate for the year ahead given that there had been some increase in medium-term inflation risks. The Reserve Bank will need to carefully monitor the balance of risks for the economy in the period ahead.

In the year ahead, headline CPI inflation will also be boosted by the impact of the government's tax reform package. Because some of the tax reductions in the package do not take effect immediately, the first-year effect on the price level is likely to be larger than the long-run effect. Altogether, the net price-level effect of the package could possibly amount to 2¾ per cent in the first year of implementation. The Reserve Bank has indicated that it will look through this 'first-round' effect in formulating monetary policy, but it will need to resist any tendency for one-off price effects to flow on into ongoing inflation.

Fiscal policy

The focus of fiscal policy in recent years has been on consolidation and on establishing an institutional framework that is more supportive of ongoing prudent fiscal management. The general government budget balance has improved markedly since the mid-1990s and is now broadly in balance. At the Commonwealth level of government, a medium-term framework for fiscal policy was set out in 1996 in the Charter of Budget Honesty and became law in 1998. This obliges the Commonwealth government to lay out its medium-term fiscal strategy in each budget together with its shorter-term fiscal objectives and targets. The strategy and objectives must be based on principles of sound fiscal management, as outlined in the Charter.[27] The other major institutional change has been the introduction of accrual budgeting. This enhances transparency by providing a more accurate view of the total activity of government and its long-term effects. In particular, it supports the principles of sustainability and sound fiscal management expressed in the Charter. The Commonwealth's 1999-2000 Budget was the first to be prepared using an accruals framework. The States and Territories are also introducing accrual budgeting – only two of the seven States and Territories are yet to present their budgets on this basis.

The Commonwealth's medium-term fiscal strategy is to achieve fiscal balance, on average, over the course of the economic cycle. This is to ensure that, over time, the Commonwealth makes no net call on private sector saving and so does not directly contribute to the national saving-investment imbalance (i.e. the current account deficit). Such a fiscal strategy enhances longer-term growth prospects, reduces Australia's vulnerability to external shocks and provides greater room for manoeuvre in response to changing economic circumstances. With the move to accrual budgeting, the Commonwealth government has slightly reconfigured its shorter-term objectives and introduced a new objective concerning net assets priorities. The revised fiscal targets are:

- maintaining fiscal surpluses over the projection period (up to FY 2002-03) while economic growth prospects remain sound;
- halving the ratio of Commonwealth net debt to GDP from almost 20 per cent in FY 1995-96 to 10 per cent by FY 2000-01;
- directing sufficient resources to high priority areas, while significantly reducing the ratio of expenses to GDP through to the turn of the century;
- no increase in the overall tax burden; and
- improving the Commonwealth's net asset position over the medium to long term.

The aim of the new objective for net assets (made up of financial and physical assets, and liabilities[28]) is to emphasise the Government's intention that fiscal policy should be sustainable and equitable in an intergenerational sense. A stronger net asset position would enable the Government to cope better with emerging fiscal pressures, notably those caused by the ageing of the population, and to meet its future obligations without requiring sharp changes in policy settings at later – and possibly less opportune – times.

Substantial progress has been made towards achieving the targets for net debt and for re-directing resources while reducing the ratio of expenses to GDP. At the same time, tax revenue as a share of GDP has remained broadly constant since FY 1996-97.[29] The Commonwealth's 1999-2000 Budget is compatible with the objective to maintain fiscal surpluses over the projection period and this contributes towards furthering the new target concerning net assets. Given that this budget has been presented on an accruals basis for the first time, the detailed discussion of the budget is preceded by an outline of the main features of the new accruals system.

Accrual budgeting

As in the private sector, the use of accruals accounting means that transactions are recorded when income is earned or expenses incurred rather than at the time that payments are made or received. For example, tax revenues are recorded in the accruals framework when tax liabilities are assessed rather than at the time that taxes are actually paid, as in the cash framework. The main advantage of the accruals framework is that it provides a more comprehensive indication of the total activity of the government and the long-term effects of government policy. This contributes to fiscal transparency, accountability, sustainability and sound fiscal management, as required by the *Charter of Budget Honesty* Act 1998. The move to accrual budgeting is also central to public sector reforms aimed at achieving better value from public expenditures. For the first time, the full cost of providing Commonwealth services is apparent and public service managers are being held accountable for the performance of their agencies in contributing to the achievement of government outcomes. It is also easier now than in the past to compare the cost of internal provision of services with the cost of outsourcing. Even so, cash measures will continue to be compiled as they are useful for tracking expenditures within the fiscal year and for assessing the short-term effects of fiscal policy on the economy.

The Government's principal indicator in the new framework is the "fiscal balance". This is the accrual equivalent of the underlying cash balance. The fiscal balance measures government net lending (saving minus investment). The main policy interest of this measure is that it shows government's contribution to national net lending and hence, to the current account balance. The fiscal balance can be derived from the "operating result" (revenue minus expenses, as in business accounts) by making two adjustments. The first adjustment is to add net capital expenditure to the operating result and remove depreciation charges. This adjustment is made to capture government investment. The second adjustment is to remove from the operating result revaluations (of assets and liabilities) as they do not affect government net lending. These adjustments are shown in Annex I. The main differences between the cash- and the accruals systems are set out in Box 1.

The Commonwealth budget

The Commonwealth fiscal balance continued to strengthen in the past year, rising from a small deficit in FY 1997-98 to a surplus of A\$ 3.1 billion (0.5 per

Box 1. Differences between cash and accruals*

Under a cash system, transactions are recorded in the reporting period in which cash changes hands. By contrast, transactions are recorded under an accrual system in the period in which income is earned or expenses incurred, provided that the transactions can be reliably measured at the time. The main differences between cash budgeting and the accrual framework are outlined below.

Superannuation

Accruing superannuation expense is recorded under accrual budgeting whether or not the liability is funded. In a given year, superannuation expense in the operating statement is equal to the superannuation accruing to current employees as well as the interest or growth of the outstanding liability. By contrast, under the cash system, superannuation outlays are only recorded when payments are made.

Public debt interest (PDI)

Under cash accounting, PDI is recorded as the interest paid during the year. Under an accrual approach, allowance is also made for interest accrued, but not actually paid during the period. Applying these principles to debt issued at a premium or a discount, the premium is recorded as an offset to PDI at the time of issue under the cash framework while the discount is recorded as PDI when the debt is cancelled. By contrast, both issue premiums and discounts are amortised over the life of the stock under the accounting standard framework (operating result) while in the accrual Government Financial Statistics (GFS) framework premiums and discounts are considered as economic revaluations.

Taxation revenue

Under the accrual system, revenue is recognised when the taxpayer makes a self-assessment or the tax office issues an assessment. By contrast, under the cash system revenue is recognised when taxes are paid. In effect, only two changes to current cash estimates are required. First, an adjustment for receivables must be made that recognises revenue for which an assessment has been issued but cash not yet received and that excludes cash received that has already been accounted for in receivables. Second, an adjustment is made for bad and doubtful debts.

Capital

Accrual budgeting records capital use (depreciation) in the operating statement, whereas cash accounting records capital expenditure. As noted above, the fiscal balance reflects capital expenditure, not capital use. Hence, the expense for capital use included in the operating result is netted out to obtain the fiscal balance and capital expenditure is added in.

---

* This section is based on Commonwealth Treasury of Australia (1999), *Budget Strategy and Outlook* 1999-2000, Statement 1, Appendix A.

cent of GDP) in FY 1998-99 (Table 10). This consolidation was entirely attributable to lower expenses, notably for personal benefits. A further increase in the fiscal balance is forecast in the budget for FY 1999-2000, to A\$ 5.4 billion (0.9 per cent of

Table 10. **Commonwealth budget developments**

	1997-98	1998-99	1999-2000	2000-01	2001-02	2002-03
	Actual	Budget	Estimates	Projections		
Revenue (A$ billion)	**148.2**	**153.3**	**162.8**	**150.5**	**153.8**	**163.1**
Per cent of GDP	26.2	25.9	26.3	22.9	22.1	22.1
Income tax		17.6	17.8	16.9	16.4	16.4
Indirect tax		5.2	5.2	3.4	3.2	3.1
Other taxes, fees and fines		1.0	0.9	0.9	0.9	0.9
Non-tax revenue		2.1	2.4	1.7	1.6	1.7
Expenses (A$ billion)	**154.7**	**150.2**	**157.1**	**143.8**	**148.4**	**151.4**
Per cent of GDP	27.4	25.4	25.3	21.9	21.3	20.5
Employees		2.5	2.4	2.3	2.1	2.0
Suppliers		2.0	2.2	1.9	1.7	1.6
Other goods and services		1.5	1.5	1.4	1.3	1.3
Personal benefits		10.0	10.0	10.5	10.3	10.3
Subsidies		0.6	0.6	0.6	0.7	0.6
Grants		7.3	7.2	4.0	4.1	3.8
Interest and other financing costs		1.6	1.4	1.2	1.0	0.9
Operating result (A$ billion)	**−6.5**	**3.2**	**5.7**	**6.7**	**5.4**	**11.6**
Adjustment (A$ billion)[1]	4.5	−0.1	−0.3	0.5	−0.2	−0.3
Fiscal balance (A$ billion)	**−2.0**	**3.1**	**5.4**	**7.2**	**5.2**	**11.4**
Per cent of GDP	−0.3	0.5	0.9	1.1	0.7	1.5
Underlying cash balance (A$ billion)[2]	**1.3**	**2.9**	**5.2**	**3.1**	**7.2**	**12.5**
Per cent of GDP	0.2	0.5	0.8	0.5	1.0	1.7
Headline cash balance (A$ billion)[3]	16.4	8.4	23.0	2.2	24.9	29.2
Tax package changes (A$ billion)[4]			**−0.1**	**−1.4**	**−0.5**	**−0.8**
Per cent of GDP			0.0	−0.2	−0.1	−0.1

1. Adjustments for revaluations and for capital. See Box 1 for details.
2. This is the previous cash-based indicator. It excludes net advances, which consist primarily of asset sales and net repayments of debt by the States to the Commonwealth.
3. Underlying cash balance plus net advances.
4. These changes have not been incorporated into the rest of the table owing to lack of disaggregated information.
Source: Commonwealth Treasury of Australia (1999), *Budget Strategy and Outlook*, 1999-2000.

GDP), reflecting an increase in revenue relative to expenses. The main items of revenue forecast to record strong growth in the current fiscal year are the dividend from the Reserve Bank of Australia (following further profitable interventions in the foreign exchange market) and income tax. The fiscal surplus is projected to rise further in FY 2000-01, to A$ 7.2 billion (1.1 per cent of GDP), despite the introduction of the tax reform package (in the form initially proposed by the Government) in July 2000. This occurs because the extra cash budget costs of this package (A$ 4.8 billion[30]) are more than offset by the one-off gain in accrued tax revenue resulting from the move to Pay-As-You-Go (PAYG) arrangements for company taxation. Some companies will be assessed for tax in FY 2000-01 under both the existing and the new payment arrangements, resulting in higher accrued revenue in that year. With the passing of this transitional effect, the fiscal balance is projected to fall back in FY 2001-02 to around the same level as in FY 1999-2000.

Revenue and expenses are projected to decline markedly in FY 2000-01, when the new Commonwealth-State funding arrangements in the tax package come into effect. These entail the abolition of Financial Assistance Grants to the States and of the Wholesale Sales Tax, reducing Commonwealth expenses and revenue, and increased expenses arising from the Commonwealth's transitional Guarantee payments to the States. The phased implementation of some of the measures in the tax package underlie the subsequent small declines in revenue and expenses as a share of GDP.

The Commonwealth underlying cash balance, the previous main indica- tor, is broadly similar to the fiscal balance except in FY 1997-98, before Common- wealth payments in respect of accumulated public trading enterprise pension liabilities[31] were incorporated in the underlying cash balance, and FY 2000-01 to 2002-03, reflecting the move to PAYG for company taxation. As companies are allowed to defer payment of part of their accrued tax liabilities in FY 2000-01, the underlying cash balance is lower than the fiscal balance in that year but higher in the following two years.

Owing to changes in the tax package that were required to get the Senate's approval, the Commonwealth's budget surpluses are likely to be a little smaller than provided for in the 1999-2000 Budget. These changes reduce govern- ment budget balances by A$ 1.4 billion (0.2 per cent of GDP) in FY 2000-01 and by somewhat less in the following two years (see Table 10 and, for more details, Table 16). As the Commonwealth government guaranteed States and Territories that the tax package would not worsen their budget positions, all of these addi- tional budget costs will fall on the Commonwealth. Taking into account these extra budget costs, the outlook is for the fiscal balance to be unchanged in FY 2000-01, to deteriorate somewhat in the following year but to strengthen subsequently. By contrast, the underlying cash balance is forecast to decline by 0.5 per cent of GDP in FY 2000-01 but to rise subsequently.

The prospects for States/local government and general government finances[32]

Adjusting for the initiatives by the governments of New South Wales and Victoria to fund unfunded superannuation liabilities, the underlying cash surplus of the State/local sector is estimated to have been around 0.2 per cent of GDP in FY 1998-99,[33] broadly unchanged from the previous year (Figure 19). A surge in capital outlays in most States was compensated for by buoyant revenue growth (Figure 20). Grants from the Commonwealth grew by a little under 7 per cent, while State's own-source revenue grew by just over 4 per cent, in line with the

Figure 19. **Underlying budget balances**[1, 2, 3]
As a per cent of GDP

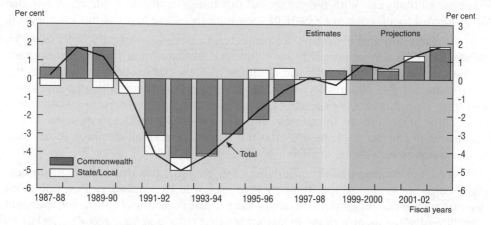

1. Budget data in "underlying terms" exclude net advances, which consist primarily of assets sales and net repayments of debt by the States to the Commonwealth.
2. Fiscal year begins on 1 July of the year indicated.
3. Cash basis.
Source: Commonwealth Treasury of Australia.

growth in current outlays. In aggregate, the States are forecasting a decline in the underlying cash balance to a small deficit in FY 1999-2000. The negative budgetary impact of rising current outlays and falling non-tax own-source revenue is forecast to outweigh a decline in capital outlays and growth in tax revenue and Commonwealth grants. On current policies, the underlying cash balance is projected to rise slightly through to FY 2001-02 as outlays to fund unfunded pension liabilities decline. Overall, adjusting for these outlays, changes in the budget balances of the State/local government sector have been small and are forecast to remain so. The outlook for the sector is broadly to remain near budget balance.

Taking all levels of government together, the general government underlying cash balance is estimated to have deteriorated somewhat in FY 1998-99 to a small deficit. A significant improvement in FY 1999-2000 is forecast in government budgets. Following a small deterioration in the following year, when the tax package is introduced, further improvements are projected in subsequent years. In order to assess the short-term effect of fiscal policy on the economy, it is necessary to make a number of adjustments to these projections. First, the deterioration in the Commonwealth cash balance in FY 1998-99 associated with the inclusion for the first time of payments in respect of outstanding superannuation liabilities of public enterprises should be abstracted from as this has no short-term effect on the economy. These payments were already being made

Figure 20. **Revenues and underlying outlays**[1, 2, 3]
As a per cent of GDP

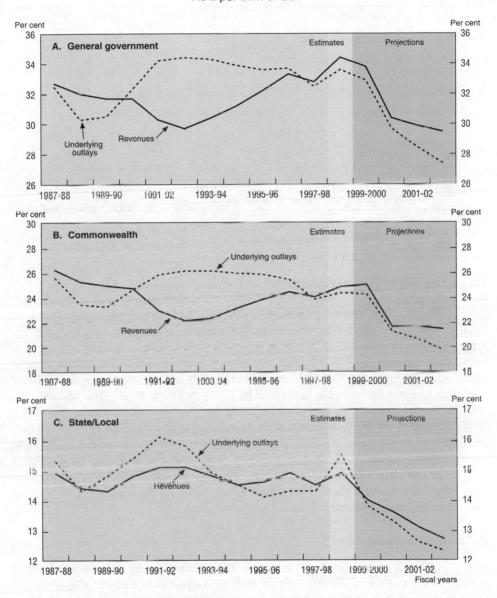

1. Fiscal year begins on 1 July of the year indicated.
2. These figures do not take account of developments since the 1999 Commonwealth Budget.
3. Cash basis.
Source: Commonwealth Treasury of Australia.

Table 11. **Changes in the general government underlying cash balance**

Per cent of GDP

	1998-99	1999-2000	2000-01	2001-02	2002-03
1999-2000 Commonwealth and State budgets	−0.4	1.1	−0.2	0.7	0.5
Outstanding Commonwealth Superannuation liabilities from public enterprises	0.2	0.0	0.0	0.0	0.0
State funding of superannuation	0.8	−0.7	−0.1	0.0	0.0
Additional cost of tax package	0.0	0.0	−0.2	0.1	0.0
Total	0.6	0.4	−0.5	0.8	0.5
Cyclical component[1]	0.3	−0.2	0.0	0.0	0.0
Structural component	0.3	0.6	−0.5	0.8	0.5

1. Assuming that the trend rate of growth equals the long-term average, 3½ per cent. The semi-elasticity of net lending as a percentage of GDP with respect to cyclical growth is estimated to be 0.37 (OECD, forthcoming).
Source: Commonwealth Treasury of Australia and OECD Secretariat.

before the change, but were recorded below the budget line. Second, the initiatives in New South Wales and Victoria to fund unfunded superannuation liabilities should be abstracted from as again there is no effect on private sector incomes. Finally, allowance should be made for the additional costs of the tax package actually being implemented. Allowing for all of these factors, the general government cash balance rises in all years except FY 2000-01, when the tax package is introduced (Table 11). Of the increase in the cash balance in FY 1998-99, about one half is estimated to be attributable to cyclical growth.[34] By contrast, the forecast improvement in the cash balance in FY 1999-2000 occurs despite a deterioration in the cyclical component. In subsequent years, the cyclical component of the cash balance is zero as growth is assumed to be at the trend rate. Overall, fiscal policy is estimated to have provided a light brake to economic activity in the past two years, to shift to a moderately stimulatory influence next year, when the tax package is introduced, but once again to have a restraining influence on economic activity in subsequent years.

Public debt developments[35]

General government net debt has fallen sharply in recent years as a share of GDP, from a peak of 25 per cent in 1995 to 14 per cent in 1999 (Figure 21).[36] Most of this reduction reflects privatisation proceeds, which in general have been used to retire debt. Had movements in net debt outstanding only reflected underlying cash balances over this period, net debt would have declined much less, to 22 per cent of GDP in 1999. The decline in net debt as a share of GDP over

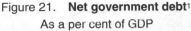

Figure 21. **Net government debt**[1]
As a per cent of GDP

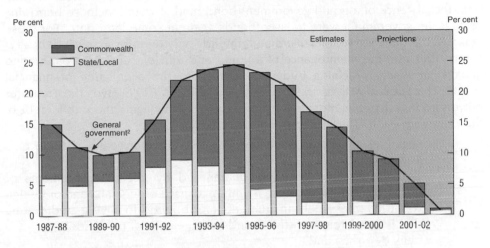

1. Debt as at 30 June as a percentage of GDP in the fiscal year ending 30 June.
2. Plus universities.
Source: Commonwealth Treasury of Australia.

this period has been similar for the Commonwealth and the States, reducing Commonwealth net debt to 12 per cent of GDP in 1999 and State net debt to 2 per cent of GDP. General government net debt is projected to continue to decline over the next few years, falling to around 1 per cent of GDP in 2003. Privatisation proceeds are expected only to account for about one third of this reduction as a share of GDP. Most of this decline in net debt relates to the Commonwealth, which is projected to eliminate its net debt by 2003. The projections for general government may well be an underestimate as they abstract from State privatisation proceeds.

Financial assets of the general government sector were about 9 per cent of GDP in 1995, when net debt peaked, and have since declined slightly to 8 per cent of GDP in 1998 (the latest year for which data are available). Concomitantly, gross debt has declined a little more than net debt, falling to 25 per cent of GDP in 1998. This is low by international comparison. Were governments to apply all of their budget surpluses (including privatisation proceeds) to reducing gross debt over the next few years, it would fall to about 9 per cent of GDP by 2003. For its part, the Commonwealth government is concerned that such an approach to debt management could render the government bond market illiquid, impeding the functioning of the private bond market. For example, the government bond and bond futures markets provide a means by which syndicate underwriters can hedge their interest-rate exposure while a new issue is being launched. In addition, the absence of a liquid government bond market would increase borrowing costs if the government were to issue bonds again at some later date. For these reasons, the Commonwealth government intends only to retire so much debt as is compatible with the maintenance of a liquid and efficient Commonwealth bond market, applying remaining budget surpluses to the acquisition of financial assets. The *Financial Management Legislation Amendment Act* 1999 gives the Treasurer powers to invest public monies for the purpose of managing the public debt of the Commonwealth. These investments may be in:

- securities issued or guaranteed by the Commonwealth, a State or a Territory;
- debt instruments issued or guaranteed by foreign governments or financial institutions whose members consist of Australia and/or foreign countries (these debt instruments are required to have a credit rating that is consistent with the sound management of public debt);
- bank deposits; and
- other forms of investment prescribed by regulation.

Assessment

With the introduction of accrual budgeting, the Commonwealth Government has now completed the reform of fiscal institutions that began with the Charter of Budget Honesty in 1996. Fiscal policy is now more transparent than ever before and more useful information is available both to policy makers and to markets. In accordance with the requirements of this institutional architecture, fiscal policy has a medium-term focus and is consistent with the principles of sound economic management, as outlined in the Charter. In view of Australia's relatively large structural current account deficit, the Commonwealth Government has established the prudent aim of maintaining budget balance over the course of the cycle so as not to contribute directly to this deficit. This implies running budget surpluses in the advanced stages of the economic cycle. Although there is always uncertainty as to how long a business cycle will last, the present cycle in Australia is now about eight years old, which is an advanced age by historical standards. Accordingly, the Commonwealth Government's shorter-term target of maintaining budget surpluses over the next few years, while growth prospects remain favourable, is compatible with the medium-term objective of balance over the cycle. While the underlying cash surplus will decline in FY 2000-01, when the tax package is introduced, the fiscal stimulus to the economy will nevertheless be modest and, on current policy settings, will be reversed in the following year. Tax reform was always going to come at a budget cost and, with the economy slowing, the timing of this modest stimulus should not present major problems for macroeconomic management. Australia's monetary policy regime retains the flexibility to provide an offset to the stimulus should that be required.

Maintaining budget balance over the cycle implies a steadily improving net asset position for the government over time. Indeed, in contrast to most other OECD countries, the Australian government is now in a position where it must decide how to allocate the improving net debt position between reducing gross liabilities and accumulating financial assets. Given that there appear to be a range of economic benefits from maintaining a liquid government bond market, the Government's decision to retire only so much debt as is compatible with maintaining a liquid government bond market, and for further reductions in net debt to reflect rising financial assets, seems reasonable.

The Government's present strong fiscal position and medium-term fiscal framework should help to reduce disruption associated with meeting the budget costs of population ageing and the government's obligations, notably for unfunded public sector pensions, which are not included in debt data and which, for all levels of government, amounted to a liability of 23 per cent of GDP in 1998. Such a fiscal strategy, together with modest budget costs of population ageing, mean that Australia is much better placed to meet medium-term fiscal challenges (notably associated with population ageing) than are most other OECD countries. The medium-term fiscal framework should help to limit the risks of fiscal slippage over the period ahead, and it will be particularly important that such slippage does not occur if Australia is to maintain its present sound fiscal position.

III. Progress in structural reform

For much of this century, economic institutions in Australia developed around the idea of redistributing rents from the rich primary commodity sectors to the rest of the economy. Key features of these arrangements were high import protection, notably for the manufacturing sector, and a centralised wage setting system that fixed a multitude of legally-binding minimum terms and conditions for employment relationships. Anti-competitive arrangements in a variety of other sectors, such as the major infrastructure industries, also yielded rents for their owners and workers. While these institutions appear to have been effective in redistributing wealth away from the primary commodity sectors, they were unsustainable because the primary commodity industries have been progressively shrinking relative to the rest of the economy and commodity prices are in long-term decline. In addition, such arrangements were having a pernicious effect on living standards by wasting resources in sectors in which Australia did not have comparative advantage and by weakening competitive pressure to raise productivity. Rapid economic development in Asia only served to accentuate these costs.

The first break with this model came in the 1970s, when major reductions in import tariffs were made, especially for manufactured goods. After a pause, phased tariff cuts recommenced in the early 1980s and are still occurring. Tariffs in Australia are now lower than in most other OECD countries, including the United States and the European Union. This marked opening of the domestic economy to international competition, together with intensifying competition in the global economy, created pressure for further structural reforms to remove impediments to the competitiveness of exposed sectors. As discussed in previous issues of the OECD *Economic Survey of Australia*, there have been major reforms in labour market regulation, education and training, infrastructure industries, the public sector, product market competition and financial market regulation. An overview of these reforms, together with suggestions for further reforms, is presented in Table 12. Like the tariff reforms, these reforms have involved putting in place an institutional framework that facilitates increased economic efficiency, dynamism and flexibility. In many cases, this has involved dismantling barriers that shielded

Table 12. **Follow-up on OECD recommendations for structural reform**

Proposal	Actions taken	Assessment/recommendations
I. Increase the flexibility of wages and employment conditions		
– Make further efforts to arrive at a decentralised industrial relations system based on enterprise bargaining.	– Implementation of the *Workplace Relations and Other Legislation Amendment Act 1996* (WRA) in early 1997. Also, legislation currently before the Parliament seeks to streamline agreement-making.	– Ease regulatory requirements further so as to encourage comprehensive enterprise agreements (as opposed to "add-ons" to awards).
– Simplify the complex and prescriptive award system.	– The WRA restricts awards to 20 "allowable matters" as from July 1998, in order to confine awards to a safety net of minimum wages and core conditions of work. Also, a draft law of 1999 further reduces allowable matters and links access to safety net adjustment.	– Speed up the rather slow award simplification process and reduce the number of allowable matters further.
– Increase in award wage rates should be modest and focus on the low paid, consistent with the intention that awards operate as a safety net.	– April 1999 "Safety-Net Review" delivered a two-tiered increase in award wages, with the largest increases benefiting those on the lowest award of pay, together with a rise in the federal minimum wage of 3.2 per cent. Also, a draft law of 1999 focuses the wages safety net on basic minimum wages.	– Wage increases should better reflect the employment prospects of the low skilled.
– States which maintain award systems should harmonise their industrial relations legislation with that of the Commonwealth.	– Western Australian legislation largely mirrors federal law. South Australia introduced a Bill in 1999 with similar content to the federal law. The Commonwealth has encouraged debate about the introduction of a unified workplace relations system in Australia although it should be noted that such a proposal is not yet endorsed Government policy.	– More legislative support for the operation of the WRA is needed from other states.

Table 12. **Follow-up on OECD recommendations for structural reform** *(cont.)*

Proposal	Actions taken	Assessment/recommendations
– Reform employment protection legislation, limiting the potential costs of dismissal and reducing disincentives to hiring.	– A draft law of 1999 excludes small businesses under certain conditions from employment protection legislation. An additional draft law of 1999 further reforms employment protection legislation.	– Implement small business exclusions and consider more general reform of the legislation.
II. **Reform labour market assistance**		
– Make labour market assistance more responsive to the needs of the clients and enhance its efficiency by introducing more competition into the market.	– The employment services market (*Job Network*) commenced on 1 May 1998. It comprises more than 300 private, community and government providers of assistance.	– Make careful evaluation of reform as soon as possible.
III. **Improve the education and training system**		
– Reform industrial relations and the apprenticeship and traineeship systems to facilitate the development of vocational education and training (VET).	– The WRA provides greater scope to customise wages and employment conditions for apprentices and trainees to suit enterprise needs and to suit different types of training. Approving authorities were established to implement flexible minimum wages in agreements.	– There has been considerable growth in structural training arrangements.
	– The *New Apprenticeship Scheme* was introduced in 1997. It is based on the old scheme but is simpler, more relevant, more flexible and more responsive to the needs of users.	– VET is becoming better adapted to client needs.
	– Considerable progress has been made in developing training packages, which are sets of competency standards aligned to the *Australian Qualifications Framework*. They are the foundation stone for the development of a private training market.	– The training market is developing steadily.
		– There is scope to increase competitiveness in higher education.

Table 12. **Follow-up on OECD recommendations for structural reform** *(cont.)*

Proposal	Actions taken	Assessment/recommendations
	– User choice was introduced in 1998 to create market-type conditions in the provision of off-the-job training for New Apprentices.	
	– A wage top-up for full-time apprentices and trainees was introduced in 1998.	
	– Articulation between school-based VET and apprenticeships and traineeships has been improved.	
– Increase fees for higher level Technical and Further Education (TAFE) courses to be more in line with university fees for comparable courses and introduce Higher Education Contribution (HEC) arrangements.	– None.	– Recommendation maintained.
		– Reduce the incidence of early school leaving.
		– Develop and strengthen pathways from school to work, especially for those young persons most at risk of experiencing difficulty.
IV. Enhance product market competition		
– States and Commonwealth regulators should co-operate to ensure that the National Competition Policy works effectively.	– The conduct code has now been legislated in all jurisdictions. Considerable progress has been made in the related reforms in electricity and gas with greater attention now being given to water and road transport. All legislation impacting on competition continues to be reviewed systematically. These reviews are on schedule but many have not yet passed to a policy stage. Phased payments are being made to States and Territories dependent on progress in implementation of agreed competition policy reform.	– Continue to implement the *National Competition Policy* and to make payments to States and Territories conditional on progress in the implementation of agreed reforms.
		– More progress should be made on reforms affecting small businesses, including agricultural marketing arrangements, taxi licensing, the regulation of professions and mandatory insurance arrangements.

Table 12. Follow-up on OECD recommendations for structural reform *(cont.)*

Proposal	Actions taken	Assessment/recommendations
– Enhance efficiency of the rail system, notably by developing a common standard for rail regulation establishing an access regime for interstate track and privatising the National Rail Corporation.	– The *Australian Rail Track Corporation* was established in 1997 to act as a one-stop shop for inter-state rail operators wanting access to track. The Government privatised the Australian *National Railway Commission,* which *inter alia* operates freight and passenger services. Further asset sales are planned in this context.	– Develop rail system policy in the context of an integrated land transport policy that also takes into account environmental considerations.
		– Ensure that track owners and train operators face incentives that encourage the efficient development of the rail system.
	– The Commonwealth is working with the rail industry and State and Territory governments to establish a mechanism for standardising rail operations. This includes establishment of the Australian Rail Operations Unit on 1 January 2000 which will publish codes of practice for rail operations (now being drafted). Implementation of the codes is scheduled for mid-2000.	– Implement the process agreed by the Australian Transport Council to harmonise interstate operational regulations.
		– Review the intergovernmental agreement on mutual recognition of safety accreditation.
		– Sell *National Rail,* the main interstate freight operator, as agreed in principle by governments.
– Establish a tariff reduction programme for the period beyond 2000, when the present programme expires.	– None since the decisions in 1997 to freeze tariffs on cars at 15 per cent from 2000 until 2005, and then cut them to 10 per cent and to have a broadly similar pause for the textile, clothing and footwear industries.	– Recommendation maintained.
– Make large cuts in the high tariffs for cars, footwear, clothing and textiles.		– Recommendation maintained.

Table 12. **Follow-up on OECD recommendations for structural reform** *(cont.)*

Proposal	Actions taken	Assessment/recommendations
V. Reform the health care system to achieve social objectives more efficiently		
– Generalise the use of casemix funding (*i.e.* payment for a treatment episode on the basis of average expected costs) in public hospitals and outpatient departments.	– All States except NSW use casemix for funding acute inpatients. Casemix funding has been extended to public outpatient departments (Ambulatory) in Queensland, Victoria, South Australia and the ACT. It is understood that this has not yet occurred in the other States and Territories.	– Generalise the use of casemix funding in public hospitals and their outpatient departments in the States and Territories where this has not yet occurred.
– Develop more arrangements for limiting the use of fee-for-service-payment arrangements for medical services.	– Co-ordinated care trials are underway and, if successful, could lead to a further reduction in unnecessary servicing. The final evaluation report is due in June 2000.	– Recommendation maintained.
	– Total outlays payable through some components of the Medicare Benefits schedule have been capped. The Commonwealth Government has entered agreements with the profession to cap total outlays in respect of pathology, diagnostic imaging and general practice.	
– Replace community rating by lifetime community rating (where persons taking out health insurance later in life pay higher premiums than those who take it out earlier).	– Lifetime community rating will come into effect in July 2000.	
VI. Reforms to cope with population ageing		
– Raise the preservation age for superannuation benefits to that required for access to the age pension (*i.e.* 65).	– None.	– Recommendation maintained.

Table 12. **Follow-up on OECD recommendations for structural reform** (cont.)

Proposal	Actions taken	Assessment/recommendations
– Limit the value of owner-occupied housing that is exempt from the means (assets) test for the age pension.	– None.	– Recommendation maintained.
VII. Reform the tax system		
– Replace Whole Sales Tax (WST) by general consumption tax.	– In July 2000, the WST will be abolished and a goods and services tax (GST) will be introduced.	
– Reduce high effective marginal tax rates and alleviate poverty trap problem.	– The tax package also reduces marginal income tax rates for most taxpayers. In addition, there will be large reductions in marginal effective tax rates.	
– Abolish inefficient state indirect taxes.	– These are to be abolished. Abolition of the debits tax has been deferred until 2005.	– The additional delay in abolishing the debits tax reduces the efficiency gains from the tax reform package.
– Reform the States' narrow-based payroll tax and determine the role of environmental taxes in achieving ecological objectives.	– None.	– Recommendation maintained.
VIII. Reform the financial system to increase competition and to improve efficiency		
– Implement second and final stage of financial system reforms. This transfers regulatory responsibility for building societies, credit unions and friendly societies to the Commonwealth government.	– Second stage changes have now been implemented. Regulatory responsibility for these financial institutions has now passed to the Commonwealth institutions charged with financial market regulation.	
IX. Reform regulation to improve corporate governance		
– Implement fully the Corporate Law Economic Reform Programme (CLERP).	– The CLERP Bill, which implements reform proposals in relation to takeovers, fundraising, Directors' duties and accounting standards, has been passed by the Parliament and is expected to come into effect on 13 March 2000.	– Implement the reforms relating to the regulation of financial markets and products (CLERP 6) and to reducing the paper compliance burden on Australian companies (CLERP 7).

Source: OECD Secretariat.

businesses and individuals from competition. The comprehensiveness, consistency and credibility of structural reforms have underpinned a shift in economic culture from rent seeking to value creating.

The benefits of such an approach to structural reform have become apparent in Australia's improved productivity performance, which is discussed in the following section. This performance also testifies to the generally high quality of the reforms. The remainder of the chapter focuses on recent progress in structural reform in the labour market, education and training, product market competition and tax reform. These reforms are central to the overall programme and are likely to have significant, beneficial effects on Australia's economic performance.

Productivity growth has strengthened[37]

At the heart of Australia's "miracle economy" in recent years has been a surge in productivity growth to rates that are high by both international and historic comparison. Total factor productivity growth (TFP), which measures growth in output not accounted for by growth in factor inputs, has increased in the market sector[38] from an annual rate of 1.1 per cent in the previous productivity cycle[39] (1989-94) to 2.4 per cent in the latest cycle (1994-98) (Table 13).[40] This is much higher than the long-term (1965-98) average of 1.4 per cent. Trend productivity growth is now at an historical high, having surpassed the high rates recorded in the late 1960s and early 1970s (Figure 22).[41] The same patterns are evident for

Table 13. **Productivity growth**[1]

Average annual growth rate

Productivity cycles	Labour productivity[2]	Capital productivity	Total factor productivity	Capital labour ratio
1964-65 to 1968-69	2.5	−1.8	1.3	4.5
1968-69 to 1973-74	2.9	−1.5	1.6	4.5
1973-74 to 1981-82	2.4	−1.8	1.3	4.3
1981-82 to 1984-85	2.3	−1.8	1.2	4.2
1984-85 to 1988-89	1.0	0.3	0.8	0.7
1988-89 to 1993-94	2.0	−0.7	1.1	2.8
1993-94 to 1997-98	3.2	0.8	2.4	2.4
Long-term				
1964-65-1997-98	2.3	−1.0	1.4	3.4

1. Market sector. This covers sectors in which outputs are valued in the market. It covered 61 per cent of GDP in 1997-98.
2. Per hour worked.
Source: Australian Bureau of Statistics.

Figure 22.   **Trend TFP growth**[1]
Growth over previous period

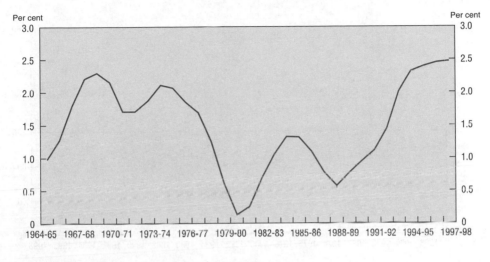

1.   Calculated using Henderson 11-period moving average.
Source: Australian Bureau of Statistics.

Figure 23.   **TFP growth by business cycle**
Percentage change on a year earlier

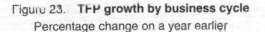
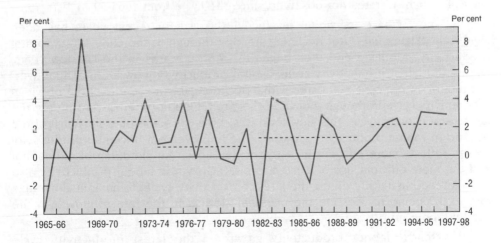

Note: Dotted lines are average TFP growth rates for business cycle periods, measured from the year following each
        cyclical trough year to the next trough year.
Source: Australian Bureau of Statistics.

Figure 24. **Capital-, labour- and total-factor productivity**
Indexes 1996-97 = 100

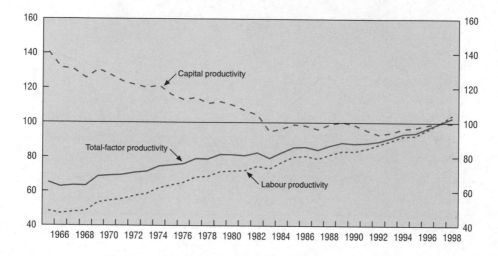

Source: Australian Bureau of Statistics.

business cycle periods (Figure 23). TFP growth has accelerated markedly during the current business cycle (which began in 1991-92, the year following the last cyclical trough) to rates not observed since the cycle from 1968-69 to 1974-75.

The increase in capital productivity growth in recent years has been significant (Figure 24). After declining steadily through to the early 1980s, capital productivity stabilised and then began to trend upwards in the last few years. During the latest productivity cycle, capital productivity grew at an annual average rate of 0.8 per cent, compared with a decline of 0.7 per cent over the previous productivity cycle. Although growth in the capital-labour ratio slowed during the latest productivity cycle, this slowdown was too small to account for much of the pick up in capital productivity growth.[42] The improvement in capital productivity growth reflects more efficient investment decisions, the shedding of old capital and the more efficient use of existing capital. Growth in labour productivity also strengthened markedly during the latest productivity cycle, to an annual average rate of 3.2 per cent, despite the marginal slowing in the rate of growth in the capital-labour ratio.

Trend[43] labour productivity growth in the latest productivity cycle increased by more than the average for the market sector in the following sectors: wholesale trade; construction; retail trade; and accommodation, cafés and restau-

Table 14. **Trend productivity growth, by sector**[1, 2]

	Constant price weight[5]	Labour productivity growth			Capital productivity growth			Total factor productivity[3]			Capital-labour ratio growth		
		1988-89 to 1993-94	1993-94 to 1997-98	Change	1988-89 to 1993-94	1993-94 to 1997-98	Change	1988-89 to 1993-94	1993-94 to 1997-98	Change	1988-89 to 1993-94	1993-94 to 1997-98	Change
A. Agriculture, forestry and fishing	5.5	1.7	1.5	-0.2	0.0	1.4	**1.4**	0.9	1.4	**0.5**	1.7	0.1	-1.6
B. Mining	7.5	6.2	5.1	-1.1	1.1	0.5	-0.5	2.6	2.0	-0.6	5.1	4.6	-0.6
C. Manufacturing	20.8	3.2	2.6	-0.5	-0.4	-0.4	0.0	**1.9**	1.6	-0.3	3.5	3.0	-0.5
D. Electricity, gas and water supply	4.5	8.7	7.5	-1.2	2.7	0.3	-2.4	4.3	2.5	-1.8	6.1	7.2	1.2
E. Construction	9.5	0.5	1.3	0.8	-1.5	-0.2	**1.4**	0.1	1.0	**0.9**	2.0	1.5	-0.6
F. Wholesale trade	9.7	2.0	3.6	**1.6**	1.5	2.2	0.8	.8	3.2	**1.4**	0.5	1.4	0.9
G. Retail trade	9.7	1.1	1.6	0.5	-1.2	-1.2	0.0	0.5	0.9	**0.4**	2.3	2.8	0.5
H. Accommodation, cafes and restaurants	3.6	-1.1	-0.7	**0.4**	-3.0	-3.3	-0.2	-1.5	-1.2	0.3	2.0	2.6	0.6
I. Transport and storage	10.6	2.0	2.0	0.0	-0.4	0.4	**0.8**	1.1	1.4	**0.4**	2.5	1.7	-0.8
J. Communication services	4.9	8.0	5.9	-2.1	-3.3	-2.1	**1.1**	2.4	2.4	0.0	11.3	8.1	-3.2
K. Finance and insurance	10.2	4.5	4.2	-0.2	0.1	0.8	**0.7**	2.5	2.7	0.2	4.4	3.4	-1.0
P. Cultural and recreational services	3.1	-0.3	-0.3	0.1	-1.9	-2.5	-0.6	-0.9	-1.0	-0.1	1.5	2.2	0.7
Market sector	100.0	2.2	2.4	0.3	0.0	0.4	0.4	1.5	1.8	0.3	2.2	2.1	-0.1

1. Trend data have been obtained using a Hodrick-Prescott (100) filter.
2. The sectors with the largest changes in total factor productivity growth are highlighted in the first column. The largest changes in each category of productivity growth are shown by bolding the figures in the relevant column.
3. Calculated using a Tornqvist index.
4. At basic prices, 1997-98.
5. Reference year for chain volume measures is 1996-97.
Source: Australian Bureau of Statistics and OECD Secretariat.

rants (Table 14). These sectors are all labour-intensive and, as such, may have benefited disproportionately from labour market reform, which has given firms greater scope to negotiate changes in working arrangements to enhance productivity. Another factor contributing to this performance is that growth in capital deepening accelerated more than average in all of these sectors, except construction. The decline in the growth of capital deepening in the construction sector contributed to it also having an above average pick up in capital productivity growth. This was also a factor in the other sectors (agriculture, forestry and fishing; and communication services) that recorded a greater than average increase in capital productivity growth. TFP growth, which can be thought of as a weighted average of labour and capital productivity growth, improved most over the latest productivity cycle in wholesale trade and construction. (An analysis of actual – as opposed to trend – productivity data by sector can be found in Annex II.)

Figure 25. **Trend TFP growth by sector**[1]
1988-89 to 1997-98

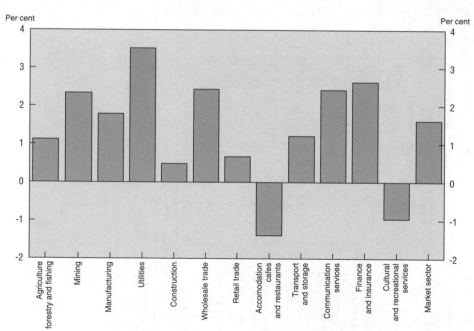

1. Trend data have been obtained using a Hodrick-Prescott (100) filter. TFP is calculated using a Tornqvist index.
Source: Australian Bureau of Statistics and OECD Secretariat.

Taking the latest two productivity cycles together, TFP growth was highest in the utilities (electricity, gas and water), finance (finance and insurance), communications, wholesale trade and mining sectors (Figure 25). The good performance in the utilities and communication sectors, which are dominated by public enterprises, is undoubtedly partly attributable to competition reform and corporatisation (see below). Sector-specific reform has also been important in the finance sector, as has been the diffusion of information technology. This latter factor also appears to have been important in wholesale trade. While labour-market reform has given firms in all sectors greater scope to negotiate changes in working arrangements that enhance productivity, this appears to have been particularly important in the mining sector.

Of the sectors that recorded above average trend TFP growth over the last two productivity cycles, all but finance and insurance and manufacturing passed this on to customers in below average increases in the trend price deflator (Table 15). Indeed, trend supply prices fell in the communications sector and rose by less than 1 per cent per year in the utilities sector, despite the strong increases in demand and output in both sectors. This suggests that competition reforms have been particularly effective in ensuring that the benefits of

Table 15.   **Distribution of productivity gains**[1, 2]

Average annual percentage change

	Price deflators	Wage compensation per hour	Operating surplus and mixed income per unit of net capital stocks
	1988-89 to 1997-98	1988-89 to 1997-98	1993-94 to 1997-98
A. Agriculture, forestry and fishing	2.4	4.3	1.4
B. **Mining**	1.2	5.1	1.1
C. Manufacturing	2.8	4.7	1.9
D. **Electricity, gas and water supply**	0.7	4.9	1.7
E. Construction	1.1	0.1	1.1
F. **Wholesale trade**	1.2	4.6	0.8
G. Retail trade	1.3	4.2	−4.2
H. Accommodation, cafes and restaurants	5.0	4.6	1.1
I. Transport and storage	2.7	5.2	1.6
J. **Communication services**	−0.9	5.3	1.7
K. **Finance and insurance**	3.8	6.6	5.2
P. Cultural and recreational services	5.4	5.8	−0.0
Simple average	2.2	4.6	1.1

1.   Based on trend data, which have been calculated using a Hodrick-Prescott (100) filter.
2.   The sectors highlighted are those with above average growth in total factor productivity.
Source: Australian Bureau of Statistics and OECD Secretariat.

productivity growth in these sectors are passed on to customers in lower prices. Wage increases and growth in profitability were above average in all of the sectors recording high TFP growth except wholesale trade and mining. All of the benefits of high TFP growth in the wholesale trade sector were passed on to customers, suggesting that competitive pressures in this sector were intense. In mining, wage increases were above average but growth in profitability was below average. Taken together, the rise in productivity growth in industries benefiting from reform made a significant contribution to lowering inflation pressures in the economy as a whole. This in turn meant continued growth in real wages, household income and consumption, and was achieved with little diminution in the growth of profits or the incentive to invest. In fact, business investment remained at high levels through the period.

Labour market policies

Industrial relations

As noted above, promoting productivity through labour market arrangements that are more adaptable to a rapidly changing economic environment has been a reform priority in recent years. A major step in this direction was the implementation of the Commonwealth's *Workplace Relations Act* 1996 (WRA) at the beginning of 1997, which sought to enhance the regulatory flexibility in the labour market by shifting the focus of workplace relations away from centrally-determined awards[44] towards bargaining of wages and employment conditions at the enterprise level. To further advance this process of workplace reform, the Government in June 1999 proposed further changes to refine and reinforce the enterprise focus of the WRA. The intention was to build on and widen the progress already made since 1997 to ensure continuing gains in flexibility and productivity.

Award simplification

In line with the objective of confining the role of the award system to a safety net of minimum wages and core conditions of work, the WRA reduced the formerly comprehensive coverage of awards to 20 "allowable matters" as from 1 July 1998. The WRA also has provision for exceptional matters orders to be made about non-allowable matters. As a result of this and other changes being made to awards through the simplification process, the award system is becoming less complex and prescriptive and more user friendly and accommodating to the varying circumstances of different workplaces and enterprises. Accordingly, the WRA restricted the jurisdiction of the Australian Industrial Relations Commission (AIRC) in the exercise of arbitration powers in respect of award-making and award-variation to the above matters.

But given the enormous complexity of the old system, the uncertainty of the involved parties about what is and is not an "allowable matter" as well as the remaining broad range of issues[45] which the 20 "allowable matters" cover, award simplification has proved a slow process: in the eighteen months from 1 January 1997 to 30 June 1998, only 121 of the originally around 3 200 federal awards were indeed simplified. In consequence, the vast majority of the existing awards continued to address issues which were no longer "allowable" and, thus, had become non-enforceable on 1 July 1998. In the twelve months to 1 July 1999, another 125 awards were aligned with the provisions of the WRA, with a further 78 awards simplified between 1 July 1999 and 30 September 1999. More than 1 000 awards are currently caught up in the simplification process. However this process should accelerate as several key award simplification decisions by the AIRC deal with the determination of a range of matters which should provide significant guidance for many other awards. Moreover, the total number of awards fell to about 2 000 as a result of awards being set aside (ie they are no longer operational), often through the award simplification process. Out of concern that the low speed of removing non-allowable matters from awards could hamper the progress of workplace relations reform, the federal Government established in June 1999 a specialist team to assist award parties with the simplification of their awards.

The Government in June 1999 sought to enhance the regulatory flexibility of workplaces by proposing changes to the WRA to advance award simplification. Under these proposals, the definitions and specifications of the various allowable award matters would be tightened and the number of allowable matters would be reduced by removing elements which duplicate other legislative entitlements or are more appropriately decided at the workplace level. These changes, if approved, would clarify the original intent of the WRA and widen the scope for better quality and more innovative agreement-making and require the individual situation of the respective enterprise to be properly taken into account.

Enterprise bargaining

In addition to reducing the coverage and complexity of awards, the *Workplace Relations Act* 1996 has expanded the opportunities for enterprise bargaining, in order to move more decisively in the direction of a simplified and highly flexible workplace relations system. To this end, the WRA provides for easier access to formalised individual agreements between employer and employees (Australian Workplace Agreements, AWAs) and to non-union collective agreements[46] (Certified Agreements[47]). Latest statistics show that the positive trend since the early 1990s towards decentralised bargaining continued, with a rising proportion of non-union collective agreements, albeit from a low level: from mid-1998 to June quarter of 1999 (the latest observation available), the AIRC approved 840 non-union certified agreements, covering over 69 500 employees.

Since the *Workplace Relations* Act 1996 came into force at the start of 1997, there have been 1 426 non-union agreements formalised, covering an estimated 148 500 employees and raising the proportion of non-union agreements in all certified agreements from 7 per cent in late 1997 to close to 10 per cent at present. As of 30 September 1999, around 73 000 AWAs have been approved by the Office of the Employment Advocate[48] and the AIRC. Some 1 695 employers have successfully used the AWA provisions of the WRA. The Government at present is seeking to further encourage the use of agreements through its proposed amendments to the WRA which include streamlining the requirements for the certification of collective agreements and simplifying the processes in the WRA for the making and approval of AWAs.

Altogether, nearly 26 500 (union and non-union) enterprise agreements have been formalised by the AIRC since the advent of formalised enterprise bargaining in the federal system in October 1991. This brought the number of employees covered by federal collective agreements to over 2.15 million in late September 1998 (the most recent data available), which represents 75 per cent of the estimated number of federal award employees or 30 per cent of all wage and salary earners.[49] In the various State jurisdictions, the proportion of award-based employees covered by State enterprise agreements ranges from nearly 36 per cent in New South Wales, to 65 per cent in South Australia and Queensland, 73 per cent in Western Australia and 64 per cent in Tasmania.

The reduction of award coverage to 20 "allowable matters" clearly supported the recent trend towards "comprehensive" collective enterprise agreements. These incorporate a wide range of provisions, many of which could not be included in awards as they are not part of the allowable matters or provide for innovative, flexible ways of working that suit both the employer and employees. Such provisions include primarily various worktime arrangements and ways to organise and carry out work, for example through job sharing and home-based work. The number of those comprehensive agreements rose more than sevenfold, from 66 agreements in 1997 to 486 in 1998.

The process of decentralisation of wage bargaining away from national awards to the level of companies clearly helped to link remuneration more closely to enterprise performance, in line with recommendations of the OECD *Jobs Strategy*. Figure 26 highlights a substantial degree of wage dispersion, reflecting the wide variety of particular circumstances across sectors and firms. Over time, and coinciding with the rising importance of enterprise agreements, wage dispersion appears to have increased. For example, the differential between the highest and the lowest quartile of the average annualised wage increase per enterprise agreement has grown from 2 percentage points in September 1992 (earliest data available) to 5¾ percentage points in June 1999 (Figure 27). In line with economic

Figure 26. **Distribution of wage agreements**
Average annual wage increase (June 1999)

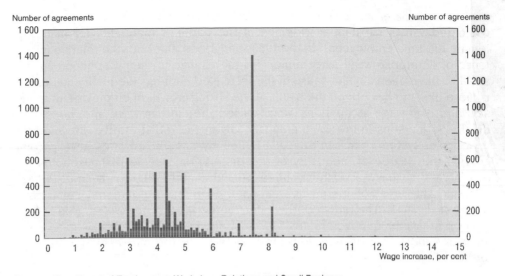

Source: Department of Employment, Workplace Relations and Small Business.

Figure 27. **Change in the dispersion of federal wage agreements[1]**

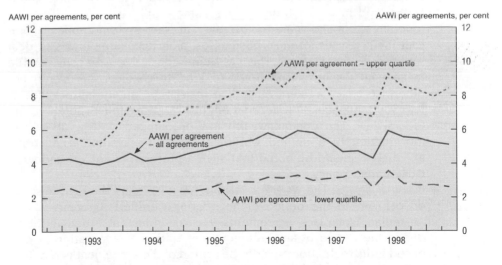

1. The figure shows average annual wage increases (AAWI) for all federal wage agreements and the upper and lower quartile of wage increases per agreement.
Source: Department of Employment, Workplace Relations and Small Business.

theory and empirical evidence, this should exert a positive effect on employment.[50]

The increased dispersion of wage agreements at the enterprise level coincided with a substantial widening of the earnings inequality for male and female full-time employees[51] in the 1980s and 1990s. But both the relative importance of enterprise wage agreements and the change in their dispersion are too small to have been a major cause of the increased earnings inequality. Instead, it is more likely to have been the result of the strong growth of employment in high skill and high wage occupations, which raised the median wage and, hence, the number of persons in low wage groups.[52] Given the redistributive effects of the tax-transfer system, which in Australia is heavily targeted towards lower-income groups, the degree of inequality of the disposable income of households has been found to have actually declined from the mid-1980s to the mid-1990s,[53] although the level of inequality remained high by international comparison (Oxley *et al.*, 1997). The redistributive effect of the tax-transfer system also helped to keep measures of poverty rates[54] for Australia below the OECD average; these measures indicate a decline from the mid-1980s to the mid-1990s (Oxley *et al.*, forthcoming).

Other areas of reform

Other major areas of industrial relations reform are the following:

- *Harmonisation of federal and State industrial relations systems:*[55] Australia has six separate industrial relations systems. The fact that most larger enterprises, and many small ones, have some employees covered by the federal system and some by the relevant state system implies significant inefficiencies for most businesses, as it forces employers to deal with two distinct systems. This has been reported to take considerable managerial resources and tends to lead to conflicts that would not otherwise arise. Western Australian legislation largely mirrors federal law. South Australia introduced a Bill in 1999 with similar content to the federal law. The Commonwealth has encouraged debate about the introduction of a unified workplace relations system in Australia although it should be noted that such a proposal is not yet endorsed Government policy.
- *Industrial disputes:* The *Workplace Relations Act* 1996 limits the right to strike or lock out to the period of negotiating Certified Agreements and Australian Workplace Agreements. Hence, industrial action is illegal during the period of an agreement's operation.[56] Notification of proposed industrial action outside the period of the agreement is required and strike pay is prohibited. The powers of the AIRC to curtail all other (*i.e.* non-protected) industrial action has been strengthened and made

enforceable by injunctions. All this has undoubtedly contributed to the continued reduction in the level of disputation in Australian work-places. In 1997 and 1998, hence after the introduction of the *Workplace Relations Act* 1996, the number of working days lost to strikes and other forms of industrial action per thousand employees, were 75 and 72, respectively, the lowest figures since this statistics started to be recorded in 1913. The level of disputes in Australia today is only around one sixth of what it was twenty years ago, when Australia was one of the most strike-prone countries in the OECD.[57] Nevertheless, during the 1990s, the number of working days lost also trended down-ward in most other OECD countries, keeping the Australian figure well above the OECD average in recent years (Figure 28). This is one of the reasons behind the Government's proposed legislation which makes sure that protected industrial action can only commence once employees have been able to express their wishes in a secret ballot and after early notification of an intention to strike. It is also planned to introduce "cooling off periods" and mediation options in circumstances where the negotiation is protracted and costly.

Figure 28. **Working days lost in labour disputes**

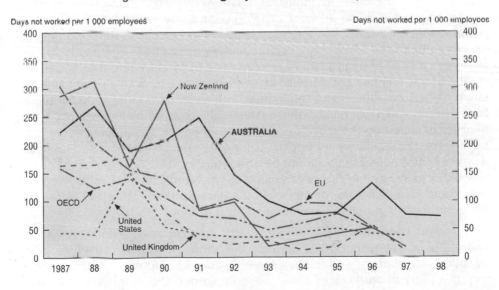

Days not worked per 1 000 employees

Source: Office for National Statistics (ONS), *Labour market trends,* April 1999 and Department of Employment, Workplace Relations and Small Business.

– *Unfair dismissal legislation*: survey evidence suggests that the operation of current unfair dismissal provisions[58] constitutes a serious disincentive to hiring workers, in particular for small firms. In consequence, the Commonwealth Government introduced on 12 November 1998 the Workplace Relations Amendment (Unfair Dismissals) Bill 1998 to amend the employment protection provisions of the Workplace Relations Act 1996. The bill proposes the exclusion of small businesses – defined as 15 or fewer regular employees – from federal unfair dismissal provisions, although the exclusion would not apply to existing employees or apprentices and trainees. The draft law also requires six months continuous employment with an employer before being eligible to lodge an unfair dismissal claim and tightens the rules governing claims by casual employees and frivolous claims. The Bill has been passed by the House of Representatives, and is currently before the Senate.

Assessment

Substantial progress has been made over the past twelve months in making the award system less complex and prescriptive and in reducing its role to a safety net of minimum wages and work conditions. Progress has also been registered in promoting the spread of collective – and to a lesser extent – of individual agreements at the enterprise level. But given the adopted evolutionary[59] approach to industrial relations reform, comprehensive agreements, which determine all work conditions and pay requirements, thus completely replacing awards, are not widespread yet. In spite of their recent fast take-up rate, albeit from a low level, comprehensive enterprise agreements continue to cover a relatively small share of employees, estimated at less than 10 per cent. In fact, a large number of enterprise agreements deal only with a relatively narrow range of work conditions and retain links with existing awards, although the key issues in the workplace relationship are generally covered by agreements. Hence, in order to speed up the move towards comprehensive agreements at the enterprise level, the regulatory requirements for collective agreements and for Australian Workplace Agreements should be eased further. The Government at present is seeking to streamline the requirements for the certification of collective agreements and simplifying the processes in the WRA for the making and approval of AWAs through its proposed amendments to the WRA.

And even though simplified awards impose fewer constraints on the operation of enterprises than before, the rather extensive coverage of the 20 "allowable matters" still implies some degree of complexity.[60] Hence, regulatory flexibility of workplaces could be enhanced if the number of "allowable matters" were reduced by more and their definitions and specifications tightened further to a less comprehensive set of core conditions of employment. As discussed above the Government is seeking approval of new legislation which addresses these issues. This would further reduce the role of awards as the benchmark against which the "no-disadvantage test" of enterprise agreements in conducted. It would widen the scope for decentralised agreement-making, taking the individual situation of the respective enterprise even better into account.

Last but not least, more needs to be done to better harmonise the operation of federal and State industrial relations systems, to reduce costs for governments and businesses. The Commonwealth should intensify its efforts to receive more legislative support from the states for the operation of the federal *Workplace Relations Act* 1999. It is noted that the Minister for Employment, Workplace Relations and Small Business has released a Ministerial Discussion Paper on the use by the Commonwealth of the corporations power under the Australian Constitution to underpin a unified workplace relations framework in Australia. The purpose of the Discussion Paper is to encourage public debate and comment on mechanisms for better harmonisation of federal and state industrial relations systems, but it is not yet endorsed Government policy. In the field of employment protection legislation, research should also be undertaken to identify to what extent the current provisions act as a deterrent to recruiting workers, in order to strike a better balance between incentives of firms to hire and the social benefits of protecting workers against layoffs.

Labour market assistance

Introducing competition into labour market assistance

The *Working Nation* labour market programme[61] – introduced in May 1994 – covered a wide range of employment initiatives which were focused primarily at the long-term unemployed, and those at risk to it. The basis of this approach was case management: jobseekers who were judged to fall into these two categories were offered individual counselling by a case manager who determined the forms of assistance necessary to help the jobseeker to get back to work. The unique aspect of case management was the introduction of competition into its delivery: a new regulatory framework was established under which case managers in the private and community sectors had to operate and jobseekers were – to some extent – allowed to choose between case managers in the private and community sectors and those in the public sector. The programme entailed a significant increase in labour market expenditures, especially on wage subsidy schemes and direct job creation.

However, this first attempt at introducing a competitive element in case management suffered from a number of deficiencies, related to incomplete supervisory powers of the regulatory authority, failure to establish a level playing field between case managers in the private/community sectors and the public sector, insufficient co-ordination among all actors, and incentives for case managers to maximise fees by referring their clients to expensive programmes rather than trying to place them in unsubsidised work. Moreover, a comprehensive assessment[62] concluded in 1996 that the overall results of the Working Nation package fell short of expectations. In particular, the decline in the number of long-term unemployed (18 months and above), although significant, turned out much lower than projected. This induced a higher proportion of job placements in so-called brokered programmes[63] than initially planned, which was particularly costly.

A new competitive market for employment services

In consequence, the new Coalition Government announced a radical reform to all areas of labour market policies in the 1996-97 Budget, which involved the most significant reorganisation of labour market assistance since the establishment of the Commonwealth Employment Service in 1946. While its focus remained on the long-term unemployed and those most at risk of joining this group, the goal of the reform was to deliver a better quality of assistance to unemployed people, to address the structural weaknesses and inefficiencies of previous arrangements, and to achieve higher cost efficiency. The Working Nation measures were wound back and expensive brokered programmes shut down. Subsequently, funding for the Commonwealth Employment Service, case management arrangements and most labour market programmes were transferred to the reformed system. The new approach gives high priority to those job seekers who are long-term unemployed or are at risk of becoming long-term unemployed. In general, the reform places more emphasis on programmes which in preceding evaluation exercises were found to be relatively cost-effective.

The main features of the reforms are the following:

– The creation of Centrelink from elements of the Department of Social Security and the Commonwealth Employment Service as the first point of contact for the majority of jobseekers, which aims at removing duplication of activities, simplifying processes for clients and improving quality of service. Centrelink provides a uniform national service for registering job seekers, administering unemployment benefits, assessing job seekers' eligibility for employment assistance, administering the activity test, and enforcing compliance with conditions of income support. It classifies job seekers, using the Job Seeker Classification Instrument (JSCI) to identify the relative difficulty job seekers have in finding employment because of their personal circumstances and labour market skills, which suggest that they could have barriers to attaining employment. Based on reference to their JSCI score, Centrelink refers job seekers with scores within a particular bandwidth to Job Network members providing Intensive Assistance. Self-help job search

facilities and basic advice and guidance over the counter are also available from Centrelink.
- The introduction of the *Job Network*, which replaces existing arrangements for labour market assistance. Job Network is a contestable employment placement market, with full competition between private, community and government contracted service providers.
- The establishment of *Employment National*, a corporatised government employment services provider, which offers services on the same terms and conditions as other service providers. In order to maintain a fully contestable market for the delivery of employment services, Employment National is required to satisfy the competitive neutrality conditions (Box 2). It also serves as a "last-resort" option in areas where the tender process fails to produce a suitable provider and this service cannot be achieved through fee-for-service arrangements. During the first Job Network contract, fee-for-service arrangements were introduced in four remote areas of Australia and there was no need for Employment National to provide services as a last resort.

The new system came into effect on 1 May 1998, replacing the fifty-year-old Commonwealth Employment Service (CES), its case management arm Employment Assistance Australia, contracted case managers, and most labour market programmes. The transition from the previous employment service arrangement to Job Network occurred within a very short space of time: 296 CES offices were closed on 30 April 1998 and replaced by around 300 Job Network members operating from more than 1 400 sites as from 1 May 1998; Job Network contracts were awarded through a competitive tender process in 1997. Special transition arrangements were put in place to transfer people in case management arrangements into the Job Network's Intensive Assistance stream. Given the scale of the reform of employment assistance, the introduction of the Job Network was accompanied by some teething problems, which required amendments during the second half of 1998. These amendments included the broadening of the eligibility for the Job Matching element of the Job Network (including unemployed people not receiving benefits) and improvements in the financial incentives for Job Network members.

Job Network members specialise in finding jobs for unemployed people, in particular for those who are long-term unemployed or at risk of it. Box 3 sketches out the array of employment services offered by Job Network members. In addition, all job seekers are able to use free of charge the job search facilities provided through Job Network Access in Centrelink Customer Service Centres.

Under Job Network, job seekers have a wide choice of organisations to help them find a job. Competition encourages a high level of service and fees paid to Job Network organisations provide a strong incentive for them to perform.

Box 2. **Competitive neutrality requirements for Government service providers**

The *competitive neutrality principle* specifies that government businesses which operate within a competitive market framework should not enjoy any net competitive advantage merely as a result of public sector ownership. This involves subjecting government businesses to the following competitive neutrality requirements:

- *Corporatisation* ensuring that significant business activities operate within an appropriate commercial structure largely separate from non-commercial activities.
- *Taxation neutrality* ensuring that the government business is not advantaged by taxation exemptions not available to other competitors.
- *Debt neutrality* subjecting the government business to similar borrowing costs as that of its competitors (by means of a borrowing charge to offset the borrowing costs advantages arising from explicit or implicit government guarantees on borrowing; or if borrowing from the Budget, requiring the Government business to pay rates of interest commensurate with prevailing financial market rates).
- *Rate of return requirements* requiring the government business to earn commercial rates of return and pay commercial dividends to the Budget.
- *Regulatory neutrality* requiring that the government businessis not advantaged by operating in a different regulatory environment to that of its counterpart private sector businesses.
- *Full cost pricing principles* ensuring that the prices charged by the government business reflect full cost allocation for its business activities.

Source: Commonwealth Government of Australia.

To ensure that highly disadvantaged jobseekers benefit from the assistance provided by Job Network, a differential fee structure applies with the highest fees being paid for those who are most at risk and hardest to place in a job. A full fee will be paid only after a jobseeker has been off allowances for longer than six months. Service providers must not refuse clients, which limits their ability to "cream" jobseekers.

In the first twelve months of the operation of Job Network over 500 000 notified vacancies were lodged on the National Vacancies Data Base compared with about 325 000 vacancies notified by the CES during the last twelve months of its existence, a cyclically comparable period. In the first eight months since the extension of Job Matching to clients who are not eligible for unemployment benefits (September 1998 to April 1999 inclusive), Job Network, on a like-for-like basis, placed 61 per cent more clients than the CES did in the September 1997 to April 1998 period.

Box 3. The Job Network

Six employment services are available under Job Network:

- *Job Matching* – gathering employers' vacancies and matching unemployed people to these jobs, including harvest work opportunities.
- *Job Search Training* – training in job search techniques (résumés, interview techniques, presentations) to prepare unemployed people to apply for jobs and give them the skills and confidence to perform well when speaking to employers; job search training is generally provided to job seekers who have been unemployed for three to twelve months and who have current work skills.
- *Intensive Assistance* – providing individually tailored help for long term unemployed and other disadvantaged job seekers to address any employment barriers and place them in jobs.
- *New Enterprise Incentive Scheme* – providing support and training for unemployed people with ideas for a viable business to help them establish their own businesses.
- *Project Contracting (harvest labour services)* – supplying labour in regions that require considerable numbers of out-of-area workers to supplement the local force in order to harvest crops.
- *New Apprenticeship Centres* – "one-stop-shops" providing integrated and streamlined apprenticeship and traineeship services to employers and job seekers; they will operate outside of Job Network from 1 December 1999.

Source: Commonwealth Department of Employment, Workplace Relations and Small Business

---

The second Job Network tender involves the delivery of employment services across Australia for the three years starting on 28 February 2000. The initiatives in the request for tender draw on the lessons learnt from the first tendering process and seek to refine the structure of incentives for bidders. For example, a bonus will be paid to Job Network members when their Job Search Training participants stay in qualifying employment for at least thirteen weeks. The past performance of bidders will be used as an indicator of success, together with the strategies outlined by a bidder, attaching a higher weight to the quality of services than to the price in the assessment of tenders.

Evaluation

A comprehensive evaluation of Job Network is underway and will be completed only in late 2001. The evaluation strategy includes an ongoing measurement of commencements in the different services available and the outcomes achieved by job seekers assisted by these services, supplemented by an analysis of trends in income support and labour force survey stock and flow data. Its main purpose is to assess how well the arrangements are working and to provide for policy adjustments over time in the light of experience. So far, a first survey of employers by the Australian Chamber of Commerce and Industry (ACCI) in late 1998 reported that employers who had used Job Network services were very satisfied with the performance of its providers, in particular compared with the former Commonwealth Employment Service. For example, the survey found that about 90 per cent of those employers who had used Job Network services would use them again. Altogether, the reform of employment assistance has generated genuine competition not only in the market for "easy-to-place" job-seekers, but also in the treatment of the long-term unemployed. Although a final assessment has to wait until the results of the comprehensive evaluation is available, it seems that this major conceptual innovation has given a boost to the effectiveness of labour market assistance.

Mutual obligation

In May 1997, the Commonwealth Government announced a labour market initiative called Work for the Dole, which seeks to involve young job seekers in a work environment, foster appropriate work habits and give unemployed young people the chance to engage with the community rather then being isolated from it. The initiative is guided by the principle of *mutual obligation* as part of the implicit social contract that underlies the income support system. The Government infers from this principle that it is fair and reasonable to ask unemployed people to participate in an activity which both helps to improve their employability and makes a contribution to the community in return for payments of unemployment benefits.[64] In July 1998, the Government built on its mutual obligation initiative by requiring all 18 to 24 year olds on unemployment payments for six months or more to undertake an additional activity such as part-time work, voluntary work, education and training, or participation in a government funded programme (including Work for the Dole).

Work for the Dole commenced as a pilot project for around 10 000 unemployed young people in receipt of income support in November 1997. Participants have to work 12-15 hours per week, depending on their age for a period of six months. In addition to unemployment benefits, they only receive A$ 10 per week in recognition of the unavoidable costs of working, such as transport to and from the project. As Work for the Dole is only a part-time work experience scheme and participants are required to continue to search for a job. Projects are focused on regions with the highest levels of youth unemployment. To avoid any displacement effect, the programme is confined to activities which do not compete with paid employment in the primary labour market.

The programme was expanded to 25 000 places a year from July 1998. Initially, the programme was targeted at people aged 18-24 years who have been unemployed for at least six months and are receiving the full rate of income support. But as from April 1999, some 6 000 additional Work for the Dole places per year were created for young people who leave school at year 12 and who have received Youth Allowance[65] for at least three months. And since 1 July 1999, the Work for the Dole scheme also has been extended to job seekers aged 25 to 34 who have received unemployment benefits for twelve months or more, as part of a wider extension of mutual obligation to that group. At the same time, the scope of mutual obligation arrangements was substantially extended, so that young unemployment benefit recipients are now able to meet their mutual obligation in 14 different ways.[66] Many of these options are not focused on immediately achieving paid employment, but rather on facilitating community engagement and developing skills, such as literacy and numeracy, that will improve the participants' long-term employment prospects. All job seekers who are in the target group are now required to attend an interview at Centrelink to discuss their options for satisfying their mutual obligation, which allows them to make their own arrangements for part-time work or to obtain an education and training place. Those who are unable to meet their mutual obligation in other ways will be required to participate for six months in a Work for Dole project. Failure to select, and then complete a mutual obligation option may result in a cut in benefit payments. The Government estimates that in FY 2000-01 more than 300 000 young unemployed will participate in one or more of the 14 options which meet their mutual obligation, among them 50 000 participants of Work for the Dole projects.

In order to assess the performance of the Work for the Dole relative to its objectives, a joint group of Government agencies conducted an evaluation of ten Work for the Dole projects during the first fifteen months of their operation.[67] The evaluation encompasses *inter alia* an analysis of the achievements of 9 400 programme participants and in-depth interviewing of a sample of about 150 respondents to measure the impact of the programme on self-esteem, motivation and work habits. Published in May 1999, the study provides an early indication of the success of the programme, particularly the widespread acceptance by programme participants, supervisors, sponsors and community members of the fairness of the scheme. The evaluation suggests that young unemployed job seekers generally expect to make a contribution to the community and appreciate the opportunity to gain valuable experience in a work environment. It turned out that three months after leaving their placement, about one-third of the programme participants had found a job. Critical comments from a minority of participants referred to the limited variety of work, that the work was not challenging enough and that it was not giving skills sufficient to get a job. Some of the critics would have preferred different work, in some cases work which used their current skills. It has to be kept in mind, however, that the case studies were based on a relatively small sample of pilot projects which may not be representative of all projects. Moreover, given the relatively short time span since the creation of the programmes there was little quantitative evidence on the longer term effects of the

Work for the Dole programme on participants and the community. The findings should therefore be used cautiously and only be considered as a tentative indicator of the wider effectiveness of the programme. A more comprehensive examination of employment and incentive effects will be undertaken later on as part of the evaluation of the extended mutual obligation arrangements. This is likely to include a net impact study of Work for the Dole.

Altogether, whether the mutual obligation programmes represent a successful shift away from passive income support to more active labour market policy depends on the extent programme participants are provided with work experience and skills valuable enough to make them attractive to employers as potential employees. The requirement that under Work for the Dole programme-jobs must not compete with paid employment in the regular labour market remains a problem as it favours unskilled work with little opportunity for training, which may impede the integration of the unemployed into gainful work.

In September 1999, the Government foreshadowed the need for comprehensive welfare reform and, to this end, has established a reference group to develop a Green Paper on welfare dependency. The group will provide advice on options for change in income support and other arrangements aimed at preventing and reducing welfare dependency. In providing this advice, particular consideration will be given to the broader application of Mutual Obligation, demographic changes, sustainability of the current system, the particular incentive effects associated with the design of the social security payments for people of workforce age, and international best practice. The Green Paper will be released for public comment early in the year 2000.

Education and training

Pressure for reform of the education and training system has come from the profound changes that have occurred in labour markets during the past two decades. Employment has shifted away from traditional core white- and blue-collar jobs in favour of jobs that require high level conceptual symbolic analytical skills or that require very little in the way of skills and training and are typically part-time or casual (Maglen and Shah, 1999). Young persons have been particularly affected by these developments. Full-time employment for young persons has contracted sharply as have real earnings for this group. These developments have increased the demand for education and training that enhances clients' labour-market prospects. The authorities have responded by undertaking comprehensive reforms to enable education and training systems to meet this demand better. The main reform themes have been developing mass education at the upper secondary level, making vocational education and training more responsive to user requirements, improving linkages between education and training and financing a major expansion in higher education in an equitable way. These issues were discussed in the 1996 and 1998 OECD *Economic Surveys of Australia*. This section discusses reforms undertaken or initiated during the past two years and suggests areas where further reform may be warranted.

Improving the quality and relevance of school education

Literacy, defined broadly to include quantitative skills, is a foundation skill for acquiring other competencies and for successful participation in the labour market, where required levels of proficiency are rising. Results from the International Adult Literacy Survey (IALS) indicate that most young Australians achieve at least the minimum level of literacy (IALS level 3) considered to be desirable to avoid difficulties in coping with social and economic life in a modern democratic society. The "document literacy"[68] results showed that the proportion of young persons that attain at least this minimum level was higher in Australia than in most other English-speaking countries but was significantly lower than in some European countries (Figure 29). While the international comparison shows that Australia is not doing too badly, the fact remains that a substantial minority of young persons does not have adequate literacy skills. This adversely affects their employment prospects (Ainley and McKenzie, 1999) and limits their scope to benefit from education and training. To address this problem, the Commonwealth government is making a significant investment in improving literacy outcomes in schools. In co-operation with State and Territory governments and non-government education authorities, it has set up the Literacy and Numeracy Programme. This supports the achievement of national goals by assisting schools to implement the agreed National Literacy and Numeracy Plan and benchmarks for minimum acceptable standards of achievement.

The Commonwealth government has also sought to improve school performance by developing national reporting on schools and by reforming funding for non-government schools. While progress in national reporting on schools has been rather limited to date, in the last year or so there have been developments that include, in particular, the 1999 agreement by Australian Ministers for Education to a new set of national goals for schooling and to set in train the development of national performance measures in specified areas of the goals, that may be followed by the establishment of agreed targets. From 1999, national reporting will include nationally comparable data on achievements against literacy and numeracy benchmarks at the primary level. With respect to the funding of non-government schools, the government has a freer hand to effect its desired reforms. As from 2001, the Commonwealth government will assess non-government schools' needs for recurrent funding on the basis of the relative socio-economic status of the (SES) of the school community. The new SES funding arrangements are intended to give low-income families greater choice in schools,

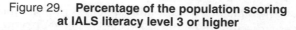

Figure 29.   **Percentage of the population scoring
at IALS literacy level 3 or higher**

On the document scale by age group 16-25 years (1994-95)

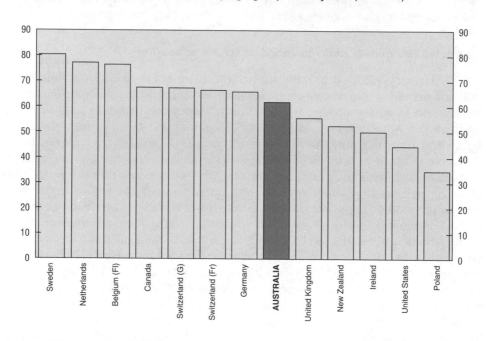

Source: OECD, *Education at a Glance,* 1998.

to encourage greater private investment in education and provide higher levels of funding for schools in the poorest communities.

Funding reforms aimed at improving performance in government schools are also occurring in some States. In particular, Victoria offers school boards the opportunity to opt for greater autonomy in running their schools through its "Schools of the Future" programme. This autonomy extends to the governance of staff, including the choice of staff and their remuneration. Audited reviews of performance occur every three years. This reform resembles those elsewhere in the public sector, where managers have been given greater autonomy along with increased responsibility for producing agreed outputs. It also puts government schools on a more even footing with non-government schools, which already enjoy such autonomy. As of mid-1999, 51 schools had opted for these arrangements.

Steps are also to be taken to update and improve teachers' skills through the "Quality Teacher Programme". The Programme will support targeted professional development activity with a focus on the renewal of teacher skills and understanding in literacy, numeracy, mathematics, science, information technology and vocational education in schools. It will target teachers who have completed formal training ten or more years ago, casual teachers and teachers who are re-entering the teaching profession. Among other programmes conducted by State and Territory jurisdictions aimed at enhancing existing teachers' skills is TRIP, which releases teachers in Victoria into jobs in the business sector (employers pay half the costs). This scheme provides teachers with general business experience, giving them a wider repertoire of skills and a better appreciation of the skills that their students will need in working life. Nevertheless, only a small minority of teachers participates in this scheme each year – about 200-300. While such schemes should make a valuable contribution to upgrading the skills of existing teachers, Australia is experiencing recruitment difficulties in some areas of secondary school specialisation such as information technology, mathematics, science and languages other than English (especially Asian languages). At the same time, the teaching workforce is ageing and there are concerns about attracting new entrants into the profession. This is reflected in the declining Territory Entrance Scores required for admission to teacher training courses. The Ministerial Council for Education, Employment, Training and Youth Affairs, which takes in all State, Territory and Commonwealth Ministers with responsibility for school education, has put in place a mechanism to monitor teacher supply and demand and established a Teacher Recruitment Taskforce. Most recently the Council has agreed to establish a taskforce to look into the skills base and qualifications of teachers graduating from university education faculties to establish whether the needs of employers are being met currently and for the future.

An important aspect of reforms to programmes in upper secondary school aimed at catering for a wider cross-section of students has been the development of vocational education. Enrolments in vocational courses have grown rapidly in recent years, with some 30 per cent of senior school students (years 11 and 12) studying at least one vocational education and training (VET) unit in 1998 (Australian Bureau of Statistics, 1999), and growth is still strong from a much higher base. In many cases, these courses include experience and learning in business workplaces. Participation in school-industry programmes has increased markedly since they were introduced, to 12 per cent of senior school students in 1996, although few students (2 per cent in 1996) participate in extended school-industry programmes (i.e. with more than 20 days in the workplace) (Ainley, 1998). Students who include VET in their school studies tend to be weaker students but to have better employment outcomes and higher participation in tertiary education than do comparable students who do not include VET in their programmes (Polesel, J. and R. Teese, 1997). Nevertheless, a comparison of school-industry programmes across States suggests that there are different approaches in the way the workplace is used to prepare young people for work. In particular, differences exist about whether programmes should be a broad generic orientation towards work or a more focused preparation for particular occupational and industry pathways. Most recent experience indicates, however, that these differences are reducing and the focus is increasingly on structured workplace learning based on the nationally recognised Training Packages which were originally developed for the post-school training sector. The Dusseldorp Skills Forum argues that these standards should include a consistent approach to the value of all VET courses and school-industry programmes and a minimum period of structured learning in all courses. In addition, programmes should be long and deep enough to deliver recognised national competencies and to lead to a recognised vocational qualification. States took a step in this direction in 1998, by agreeing only to offer VET courses in schools if they were based on national industry standards.

Training Packages, which have at their core specific work competencies, have provided a valuable structure for vocational education in schools. A difficulty, however, has been the need in most circumstances to have the competencies assessed in the workplace. The availability of suitable workplacements, particularly in rural areas and some industries has impeded progress. A further benefit of Training Packages is that they articulate directly into post-school training programmes because they are identical to the ones used in the post-school sector. This is not the case with university education, however. One of the challenges facing Australian education is the proper recognition of training, both for entry purposes for university study and as credit towards a university degree. Australian Education Ministers have sought advice from school authorities, Year 12 accreditation agencies and universities on this issue.

Improvement in the integration of VET and general education is an issue which has been taken up by Australian education ministers. Better integration would better prepare those students who enter the labour market direct from secondary school. Moreover, a better alignment of vocational education and general education would promote VET to students, and those who advise them, particularly parents.

Strengthening and expanding vocational education and training

The New Apprenticeship scheme was established in 1997. It provides competency-based qualifications that are nationally recognised. New Apprenticeships are based on the previous scheme but incorporate changes that make the new system simpler, more relevant, more flexible and more responsive to the needs of users. Flexibility has been increased by making greater provision for part-time arrangements, training arrangements of different duration and different mixes of work and training. New Apprenticeships also make possible school-based apprenticeships and traineeships, entail flexible industrial relations and are supported by a national network of one-stop New Apprenticeship Centres to support employers, apprentices and trainees. The new scheme has increased the potential use of apprenticeship-type training by expanding coverage from traditional trades (which tend to be industries with little job growth) to those industries (such as information technology, communications and services) where rapid job growth is occurring. At the end of 1998 there were approximately 220 000 New Apprentices in training – representing growth of approximately 75 000 places (over 50 per cent) in the last three years. Most of this growth has been in apprentices and trainees aged 20 or older. The proportion of teenagers participating in such arrangements has been stable in recent years (see below).

Another major policy plank in VET has been to increase the diversity of training organisations operating in the training market and to give them greater flexibility to respond to clients' needs while ensuring that training outcomes reflect industry requirements and result in portable qualifications. The foundation stone for the development of such a training market is the National Training Framework (NTF), established two years ago. It consists of the Australian Recognition Framework (ARF) and training packages. The ARF is an agreed set of standards and supporting elements that all States and Territories use to register training organisations. Training packages are sets of competency standards aligned to the Australian Qualifications Framework. They are developed by industry and bring together previously disparate approaches to standards, programmes, qualifications and learning resources. These packages provide the platform on which training providers can customise their own programmes better to meet the needs of individual clients. Considerable progress has been made in implementing training packages. By the end of 1999, it is expected that some 30 training packages covering approximately 55 per cent of the labour force will be implemented, with others still in the pipeline. There is variation in satisfaction with the current training packages across industries. Industry bodies are taking steps to review packages. Ongoing consultation with, and validation by, industry groups is an essential process in the development of Training Packages. A continual improvement process is also in place to ensure the relevance and suitability of Training Packages. For example, the first group of Training Packages endorsed in 1997 and 1998 are now being reviewed. The new framework for providing VET has proved propitious for registered training organisations, the number of which has increased from 1 200 in 1994 to over 3 800 in 1998. The overwhelming majority of these new Registered Training Organisations are in the private sector.

A key mechanism to increase the responsiveness of the VET market has been to give clients more direct choice in the quality and type of services available through User Choice. It was introduced in 1998 to create market-type conditions in the provision of off-the-job training for New Apprentices. User Choice allows employers and apprentices to select their Registered Training

Organisation, whether public or private, and negotiate key aspects of their training (including content, timing, location and mode of delivery), with public funds flowing to that provider. States and Territories allocate about 10 per cent of the total funds allocated to VET under the Australia National Training Authority Agreement (ANTA) on a contestable basis, including User Choice arrangements. One issue that affects the implementation of the competitive market principles underlying User Choice arrangements is that of low population densities in rural and some regional areas. In many of these areas, demand for VET may be unable to sustain a number of competing providers. The issue is well recognised and to some extent addressed by State and Territory governments.

The aims and directions of the VET system over the next few years are set out in the *National Strategy for Vocational Education and Training* 1998-2003. The Strategy aims to ensure that Australian workers have skills that make them highly productive. Key performance measures will be used to monitor progress on the Strategy. These are being progressively implemented, with full reporting against the measures beginning in 2001 for the year 2000. The measures will assess aspects such as how well industry needs and those of the economy are being met by the VET system, employment outcomes for students, and the relevance of training in the workplace.

The transition from school to work

For young people in Australia the process of transition from education to work, and more broadly, from social and economic dependence to independence, has undergone significant change over the last two decades. The most prominent signs of these developments are a sharp decline in teenage full-time employment and the associated rise in participation in senior secondary schooling among teenagers, an increasing combination of study and part-time work, and the rapid increase in participation in higher education. The decline in full-time employment opportunities for young people has translated into higher school participation rather than higher unemployment. Increasing opportunities in part-time work have offset some of the costs of school participation – in particular foregone income. Since the recession of the early 1990s, the picture is of relative stability in school participation and steady, if unspectacular, progress in relation to youth unemployment. ABS figures indicate that when surveyed in the year after they left school the share of young people in education increased from 54.9 per cent in 1992 to 58.3 per cent in 1998 and the share who were unemployed fell from 17.1 per cent to 12.2 per cent. The share in employment fell slightly (from 23.9 per cent in 1992 to 23.0 per cent in 1998), and the share not in the labour force increased (from 4.1 per cent in 1992 to 6.4 per cent in 1998). Moreover, the teenage full-time unemployment to population ratio has fallen considerably since the early 1990s – from around 9 per cent to around 5 per cent. Nevertheless, many young people continue experiencing difficulties, sometimes considerable, in making the transition from school to work. These difficulties may involve long periods of unemployment or engagement in marginal activities rather than attachment to the labour force that leads to constructive skills development. The experience of early school leavers and the appropriate policy response is taken up below.

As far as 20-24 year olds are concerned, the full-time unemployment to population ratio has fallen from 14.7 per cent in September 1996 to 11.4 per cent in September 1999. Moreover, the share outside full-time education and either unemployed or not in the labour force has fallen from 17.6 per cent in September 1996 to 16.1 per cent in September 1999. There is some evidence, however, that one of the impacts of increasing school participation has been to shift some of the burden of full-time unemployment from 15-19 year olds to the 20-24 year old group. This is in large part an effect of increased school participation reducing the average duration of participation in the full-time labour market by teenagers.

In the decade to the early 1990s the rate of retention to the end of secondary school more than doubled to reach a peak of 77 per cent in 1992, before falling to 72 per cent in 1998. The peak coincided with the recession of the early 1990s and the subsequent fall, which has accompanied the improving economic situation, may represent a return to a longer term trend, rather than a fall in school based factors. Despite the strong gains in high school completion, and the improving transition to work experienced by an increasing share of young people over recent years, early school leavers are a group which needs to be monitored closely. There is evidence that early school leaving is associated with a range of unfavourable outcomes. For instance, Ainley and McKenzie (1999) find that early school leaving, and low literacy levels, have a strong negative effect on employment prospects. Nevertheless, outcomes for this group are likely to vary considerably. A recent analysis (Marks and Fleming 1999) reports that, on the whole, school factors are not the main reason young people decide to leave school but that they did so to gain employment. This study found that a high share of early school leavers do find work – over 70 per cent of the sample had gained full-time work and a further eight per cent were working part time. Only about 10 per cent were looking for work. For those early school leavers who are struggling in the labour market, policy should aim to make a return to education or training attractive. At the same time schools need to be more responsive to students' needs. Measures such as improving curricula and other aspects of high school to better accommodate a wider diversity of students need to be considered. In this regard New South Wales is to introduce a revised school curriculum next year aimed at addressing the problem of early school leaving. The creation of separate senior secondary schools could also help to retain more students by offering a more adult learning style.

A new priority for guidance, counselling and career advice, especially for students not going on to university could also help to reduce the numbers of young people drifting into "at risk" situations. Should school leavers experience employment difficulties, greater monitoring and follow up would help to get them out of "at risk" situations early, before scarring occurs. Perhaps schools should be made responsible for this monitoring and follow-up, at least for early school leavers. Schools know these individuals and should have some idea about the most appropriate remedial actions to take. In addition, this would help to re-focus schools objectives, making it clear that an important objective is to assist the student in making a successful transition to adult working life. A step in this direction has already occurred in the context of the competitive employment services market. Schools are able to earn fees for placing difficult to place young persons in employment or training. Nevertheless, there is scope for schools to go further with monitoring and follow up, both in terms of helping early school leavers to find jobs (as in Japan) and of reintegrating them into education (as in the Nordic countries).

The Government's strategy is to tackle the problems of those who are experiencing difficult transitions on several broad fronts. It not only stresses the importance of improving the performance of the education and training system, but continues to give particular attention to policy for strong economic growth and labour market flexibility. With regard to young people, the strategy is to ensure that education and training systems provide the skills and attributes young people will need in the knowledge-based economy, with a focus on the achievement of minimum standards by all children. Reforms designed to widen the content of secondary school to better cater for the diversity of student needs in the post-compulsory years, and to develop alternative post – school pathways are also in place. Income support arrangements through the Youth Allowance provides incentives for young people who are not in employment to participate in education and training. In this policy environment other options have also been floated by non-government bodies. One suggestion has been for a "youth entitlement" which would give early school leavers a second chance by providing them with financial and other assistance to complete high school or gain an equivalent qualification, or obtain work which has a significant education or training component. This proposal, by the Dusseldorp Skills Forum, would set a ceiling for an individual's entitlement at the cost to government of the final two years of secondary education. Consideration of this proposal would need to take account of the incentives and programmes already in place. A positive sign is that the Government has recognised that policy development cannot stand still. The Government has recently announced a Youth Pathways Action Plan Taskforce, drawn from the community, academic and business sectors along with State and Commonwealth governments. The Taskforce has been requested to examine the most effective ways in which governments, community organisations and business can develop co-operative partnerships to strengthen and develop youth transition pathways, including pathways for those most at risk of experiencing difficulty. The terms of reference suggest that the scope of the report will not only be on the labour market and education and training, but will include other impediments to smooth transitions from school to work such as homelessness, family breakdown, and drug abuse. It is expected that the Taskforce will report early in 2000.

Employment based structured training through apprenticeships and traineeships could also have an important role to play in reducing the number of teenagers at risk of lasting labour market disadvantage. Indeed increasing young people's participation in such arrangements has been an objective of governments during the 1990s. Such structured training needs to be closely monitored to assess the extent to which young people are benefiting. While the number of adult apprenticeships and traineeships has grown, so too has the participation rate of teenagers in these forms of structured training arrangements. For example, from 1995 to 1998 the number of 15-19 year olds commencing such training rose by 38.2 per cent, and the total number in training rose by 16.0 per cent (Werner and John, 1999). This growth in teenager participation is all the more noteworthy because with increased school retention the age at commencement of those taking up these options has tended to increase.

Product market competition

Enhancing product market competition, which is a crucial element in improving economic performance, has been central to microeconomic reform in Australia. Competition in product markets has intensified as tariffs have declined and, more recently, as a result of the National Competition Policy (NCP). This was agreed between the governments of the Commonwealth, States and Territories in 1995 and is being progressively implemented. In addition to strengthening trade practice rules governing competitive conduct, the NCP extends competition into areas of the economy that have been dominated by government monopolies or where competition has been restricted by legislation. Accordingly, it affects most aspects of structural reform and, indeed, gives impetus to much of the structural reform agenda. This section reviews progress in implementing the NCP and discusses some of the challenges that lie ahead in putting into effect the remainder of the NCP reforms.

Key elements of the National Competition Policy

The NCP evolved out of a realisation that reform of competition policy was necessary to complete structural reforms already underway, notably in respect of government business enterprises, and that a nationally co-ordinated approach would deliver a more competitive national market and hence, a more productive economy. Three agreements signed by Australian governments in 1995 underpin the NCP:

- the *Competition Principles Agreement*, which sets out principles for reforming government monopolies, prices oversight of government businesses, reviews of legislation, access to some essential infrastructure facilities and placing government businesses on a competitively neutral footing with each other and with private businesses;
- the *Conduct Code Agreement*, which extends Australia's existing competitive conduct rules (*i.e.* anti-trust law) to all businesses – State Government businesses and unincorporated businesses were previously exempt; and
- the *Implementation Agreement*, which specifies a programme of financial grants to State and Territory governments, contingent on implementation of the NCP and related reforms in gas, electricity, water and road transport. These are currently estimated at over A\$ 5 billion up to 2005-06.

Two new institutions were created in connection with these reforms. The Australian Competition and Consumer Commission (ACCC) was formed mainly to administer the *Prices Surveillance Act* and the *Trade Practices Act*. And the National Competition Council (NCC) was created to assess whether jurisdictions have met their reform obligations, as well as to co-ordinate reform efforts. The reform programme was broken up into three tranches, with a major review to be undertaken before July 1997, 1999 and 2001. The NCC assesses progress against commitments for each tranche period, makes recommendations to the Commonwealth Government on the NCP payments to be made to the States and Territories. NCP payments are provided to the States as an economic dividend for their investment in NCP reform, recognising that some of the reforms are likely to increase Commonwealth revenues. The payments also ensure that at least some of the gains from reform accrue directly to the States as a fiscal incentive. The first tranche was made in full to all governments. Similarly, initial second tranche payments were made in full to all States and Territories, except Queensland, where one quarter of the first part of its payment was withheld pending a supplementary review. The second tranche non-compliance issues and recommendations are summarised in Annex III. Remaining second tranche payments will be determined following a series of further assessments to be completed by June 2000. Where issues have arisen with implementation of the reform programme, the NCC has sought to use the tranche payment assessments as a means to develop an agreed basis to progress the particular reforms.

Reform of government business enterprises

Government Business Enterprises (GBEs) accounted for 8 per cent of GDP in 1995-96, down from 10 per cent in the late 1980s, and are mostly owned by State and Territory governments. The reforms that governments are required to make to GBEs reflect similar reforms that have already occurred in some States and/or build on past reforms. The main reforms to GBEs required under the NCP are to:

- *restructure them*: Before introducing competition to a market traditionally supplied by a public monopoly – and before privatisation of a public monopoly – a structural review is required. This is required to ensure separation of potentially competitive activities from natural monopoly elements and the creation of a corporate structure for the business. Governments are able to set non-commercial objectives for their enterprises, but these Community Service Obligations (CSOs) should be clearly identified and funded. In addition, industry regulatory functions must be removed from the GBE if it has them and transferred to an independent regulator;
- *make them compete on an equal footing with private businesses*: The competitive neutrality reforms aim to ensure that GBEs do not derive a net competitive advantage from government ownership. Corporatisation is required for major enterprises. Significant GBEs must also face the same tax and regulatory regimes as private businesses, pay dividends out of profits, achieve a pre-tax commercial rate of return and pay a fee to government for the reduced credit costs that government ownership confers. Each government is required to establish administrative arrangements for hearing complaints that competitive neutrality principles have been violated;
- *establish independent price regulators where GBEs retain monopoly power*;
- *adoption of governance and accountability arrangements where the GBE is retained as statutory authority rather than as a Corporations Law company*.

The Commonwealth government and most of the State and Territory governments have largely completed these reforms. While significant progress has also been made in South Australia and Queensland, the NCC identified issues to be addressed in each of these jurisdictions. In South Australia, the NCC called for more progress in relation to smaller sized government businesses, corporatisation of outstanding significant GBEs and the treatment of CSOs (National Competition Council, 1999c). The NCC also expressed concern about the manner in which the Queensland Government rejected a recommendation of the Queensland Competition Authority regarding the means of delivery of the government's public transport policy objectives on one rail line in South-East Queensland.

Although local governments were not a party to the NCP agreements, the States and Territories accepted reform obligations on their behalf. The focus of such reforms is on ensuring that local governments' business enterprises are restructured and that competitive neutrality principles are respected. Victoria, Queensland and Western Australia have set aside a portion of their NCP payments for local governments that make satisfactory progress in implementing these reforms.

Partly as a result of competition policy, prices for the outputs of GBEs have fallen substantially in recent years, even though dividend payments to governments have doubled. In the five years to 1996-97, the sharpest price falls were in electricity (24 per cent), port services (23 per cent), telecommunications (23 per cent) and air traffic services (40 per cent) (National Competition Council, 1999a).

An emerging issue is how to reconcile CSOs with competitive neutrality requirements. Ideally, these should be identified and funded on a commercial basis directly from the government budget. This is what the ACT has done, for example, in respect of the supply of urban water and sewage services. But it is possible for a government to retain an impediment to competition to finance a CSO provided that such a course serves the overall community interest. This is what the Commonwealth government has done in respect of Australia Post's reserved services (see below). Nevertheless, such an approach is the exception rather than the rule and the NCC will only endorse the Commonwealth Government's preferred approach in this case if it can be demonstrated that an effective third party access regime is in place for Australia Post's monopoly services.

In the event that a government intends to privatise (even partially) an enterprise, it is obliged[69] to demonstrate that the competitive elements have been separated from the monopoly elements and that there is adequate, independent price regulation for the monopoly elements. Ensuring that potentially competitive elements are indeed competitive may involve splitting such elements into many entities, as occurred in the privatisation of Victoria's electricity industry (see Box 4). The only cases in which the NCC has expressed concern are in relation to Telstra (see below), the incumbent telecommunications operator, Australia National (railways) and TasRail. In the case of the two rail companies, the Commonwealth Government did not undertake the required (clause 4, *Competition Principles Agreement*) reviews.[70] However, planned future reviews may address issues in these areas.

Infrastructure reforms by sector

Much progress has been made in reforming infrastructure industries. A key feature of these reforms has been putting into effect the rules established by

---

Box 4. Privatising a competitive electricity industry: the case of Victoria

The Victorian authorities re-organised their electricity industry prior to privatisation to ensure that it would be competitive. The industry was unbundled vertically and then disaggregated. Each generating plant was put into a separate business. The businesses were broken down as far as possible without losing economies of scale. The extent of disaggregation was such that producers could not set prices. Cross ownership rules were made which prevent early re-aggregation. These rules prevent a business that owns more than 50 per cent of one of the generating companies from owning more than 20 per cent of another. Transmission lines were also privatised with access being subject to the national rules for "essential facilities". Proceeding in this way maximised the benefits for electricity customers (see below) and the economy.

---

the NCP for third party access to "essential" infrastructure services provided by facilities of national significance. "Essential" services are generally provided by networks that would not be economic to replicate. Examples include power transmission lines and rail tracks. The national access regime gives economic entities the legal right to negotiate for the use of "essential services" provided by infrastructure operated by other businesses and seeks to ensure that businesses are offered reasonable terms and conditions of access. In the event that the parties are unable to reach a commercial agreement, the regime provides recourse to compulsory and binding arbitration. This regime bears on much of the natural monopoly elements of GBEs, although increasingly these essential infrastructure services are moving to the private sector through privatisation.

Electricity

Considerable progress has been made with reforms in the electricity industry. The NCP structural reforms of electricity utilities are complete in NSW, Victoria, Queensland, South Australia and the ACT, and is well advanced in Tasmania. The National Electricity Market (NEM) commenced in December 1998, linking the wholesale electricity markets of NSW, Victoria, South Australia and the ACT. Queensland is operating a wholesale electricity market under NEM rules and will become a full participant in the NEM when it is interconnected with the NSW grid (in 2000). Tasmania will also join the NEM if an undersea power cable to the mainland proceeds (expected in 2002). The National Electricity Market Management Company (NEMMCO) is responsible for the operation of the wholesale electricity market in accordance with the National Electricity Code. The ACCC will gradually assume responsibility for regulating electricity transmission networks. There are transitional arrangements that phase in the application of the NEC pricing principles to electricity networks. These interim arrangements expire by 31 December 2002 and will cease earlier than this date in some jurisdictions.

Choice of supplier has been extended to medium-large customers and work is underway to extend this choice to all customers (expected by 2001). Savings for customers enjoying choice of supplier have been substantial. Following NCP *electricity* reform, tariffs for business users have fallen by up to 50 per cent since the levels of the 1980s. Despite a corrective upswing in 1999, a recent NUS survey ranked Australia's electricity prices as the third lowest out of 17 countries surveyed. Australian prices were about half the levels recorded in the United States.[71] Households have also benefited. The annual *electricity* bill of a typical Victorian household fell by about 15 per cent between 1993-94 and 1998-99 (Victorian Government, 1999).

Gas

Reform in the gas industry is intended to achieve free trade in gas nationwide and to develop intra-field and inter-field competition through removing regulatory impediments to trade in gas, applying access arrangements to transmission and distribution infrastructure and facilitating the construction of new transmission links between gas fields and markets.[72] The NCP gas reforms are largely complete, although some issues remain in relation to retail competition, intra-field competition and the finalisation of access arrangements in a few States (National Competition Council, 1999c). Larger customers already enjoy choice of supplier, and this is being phased in down to the household level by around 2001 in most States. Owing to a lack of competition between producers, who clean up gas and put it in the pipeline, the reforms have not had much effect on gas prices. Gas distribution tariffs, on the other hand, are set to fall by 25 per cent in Western Australia, and by 60 per cent in NSW by the year 2000 (NCC, 1999a).

Water

The NCP water reform agenda seek to address both the economic viability and ecological sustainability of the nation's water supply through a range of measures encompassing urban and rural water and industries. One area of focus has been on pricing, including establishing tradable water rights.

Irrigation accounts for a high proportion of Australia's water consumption. In general, rural customers have not being paying the full cost of the water they use, including environmental costs. Water rights have been over-allocated, leading to degradation of water supplies. To address these problems, prices for rural water are being progressively raised and tradable water entitlements, separate from land rights, have been introduced. These will enable water to be reallocated to its highest value use. They will enable producers to purchase entitlements from current users rather than obtain water by increasing diversions from already stressed water systems.

Urban water is also being priced to encourage efficient water service provision and use with a movement to two-part tariff arrangements. Residential and commercial water usage is now generally metered, users paying only for the water that they use.

Pricing reform has contributed to an 18 per cent reduction in water prices to Victorians, a 20 per cent reduction in water use in Brisbane and a fall of almost 50 per cent in real water costs for businesses in Western Australia between 1992-93 and 1997-98 (National Competition Council, 1999c).

The reforms also aim to improve water quality monitoring and land care practices to protect rivers with high environmental value. For example, governments are reserving annual allocations of water for the environment to increase native fish breeding and migration, improve bird breeding in wetland areas, and safeguard sustainability of rivers. Complementing these reforms, new investment in dams is required to involve an independent appraisal of economic viability and ecological sustainability.

Telecommunications

The telecommunications market was fully liberalised in July 1997. In line with the requirements of the NCP, regulation was separated from the commercial activities of Telstra, the incumbent telecommunications operator. Although the natural monopoly element of Telstra, the local fixed network, was not separated from the company's competitive elements, anti-competitive conduct was prohibited and third party access has been governed by a separate access regime for "essential services". On a purchasing power parity (PPP) basis, telecommunications charges by the major telecommunications carrier, Telstra, have increased slightly since 1997 for residential users but have declined marginally for business users (Figure 30). For the whole period since 1990, telecommunications charges by Telstra have remained constant in Australia but have declined markedly on average in OECD countries. Despite these trends, residential telecommunications charges in Australia are around the OECD average. However, business telecommunications charges are above the OECD average (Figure 31).

The Commonwealth government recently enacted changes to the regulatory regime governing telecommunications to limit possible anti-competitive behaviour arising from Telstra's local fixed network monopoly. The telecommunications competition regime introduced in 1997 is to be reviewed next year.

Postal services

Following the NCC's review of the *Australian Postal Corporation Act* 1989, the Government announced a package of reforms that will increase competition in

Figure 30. **Business and residential tariff basket trends**[1]
Index 1990 = 100

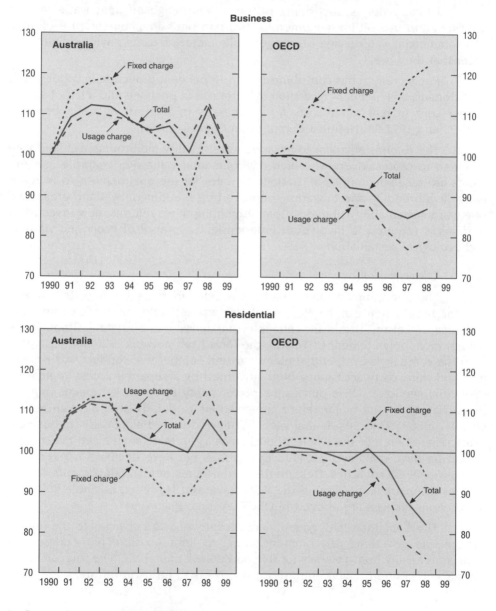

1. Data are derived using PPP exchange rates.
Source: OECD, *Communications Outlook,* 1999.

Figure 31. **An international comparison of performance indicators in telecommunications**

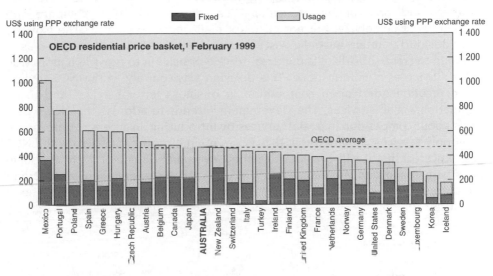

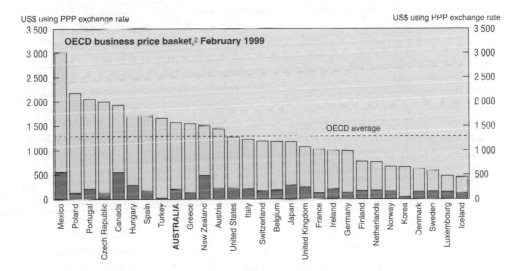

1. Including VAT. The usage charge includes a basket of 1 274 calls.
2. Excluding VAT. The usage charge includes a basket of 4 426 calls.
    For a full description of the tariff comparison methodology for these baskets, see OECD, ICCP Series No. 22: "Performance Indicators for Public Telecommunications Operators".
Source: OECD, *Communications Outlook 1999.*

postal delivery services. These reforms, which come into effect in July 2000, introduce open competition on price and delivery for mail weighing more than 50 grams and for incoming international mail and the ability to compete with Australia Post on service, but not price, for mail below 50 grams.[73] The Government decided to retain Australia Post's reserved services below 50 grams so as to continue to cross-subsidise its universal service obligation to provide nation-wide letter service at a uniform price. This decision was contrary to the NCC review, which recommended open competition in business letter services and in all international mail services. The Government intends to address the NCC's concerns about competition in postal services by introducing an access regime for the monopoly services. Provided that this access regime proves satisfactory, the NCC has indicated that it will consider that the Government has met its NCP obligations with respect to Australia Post. A review will be undertaken in 2002 and released in the following year to assess the effects of these changes and the need for further reform.

Land transport

The 1995 NCP agreements oblige governments to standardise regulations covering the road transport industry so as to facilitate national competition but do not contain a clear reform agenda. Key reforms in 1997-98 included the introduction of nationally agreed uniform arrangements for the transport of dangerous goods and a national approach to the enforcement of roadworthiness. In December 1998, governments endorsed a reform package that includes a nationally consistent regulatory framework for heavy vehicle registration, driver licensing, heavy vehicle mass and loading restrictions, commercial driver fatigue management and the national exchange of vehicle and driver information. It is now up to individual governments to put these reforms into effect. The NCC will assess them on their progress in this regard in the second tranche supplementary assessments.

Governments agreed in early 1997 to establish the Australian Rail Track Corporation to act as a one-stop shop for interstate rail operators wanting access to track. This step is intended to increase competition and contestability in the industry. The Australian Rail Track Corporation is negotiating access arrangements for the track that it does not already own and will then be lodging an undertaking with the ACCC seeking endorsement of its own access regime. In addition, the Australian Transport Council has agreed a process to harmonise interstate operational regulations and to review an intergovernmental agreement on the mutual recognition of safety accreditation. Another step that should contribute to increased competition and efficiency is the in-principle agreement by governments to sell National Rail, the main inter-state freight operator.

While these reforms go in the right direction, there remains a need to develop an integrated land transport policy. Progress in developing a more efficient road/rail transport system may be aided by removing funding imbalances that may disadvantage rail compared to road. In addition, the environmental and social costs of road transport are not adequately born by the industry (Productivity Commission, 1999), which may result in over-use of this form of transport compared to rail.

Legislation review

Governments are required to review all anti-competitive legislation to remove regulations that restrict competition unless they are demonstrated to be in the public interest and the objectives of the legislation cannot be obtained in another way. Almost 1 700 separate Acts or Regulations were identified for review. Overall, about one half of the reviews on governments' agendas have been completed or are underway, while only around 20 per cent of the reform agenda is complete; the state of the review programme is summarised in Table A5, Annex III. Redundant legislation has been repealed[74] and legislation has been amended to reflect NCP principles. Some restrictions on competition in some professions have been removed in some States. For example, the legal profession's monopoly on conveyancing has been removed in NSW and Victoria. This, together with the removal of price scheduling and advertising restrictions, contributed to a 17 per cent fall in conveyancing fees in NSW between 1994 and 1996. There have also been a number of reforms mainly focussed on the health sector in Victoria that have reduced unnecessary restrictions on commercial activities, notably concerning advertising and the ownership of practices.[75] The reviews have also led to decisions to terminate or reform some statutory marketing arrangements (barley in Victoria and South Australia, rice in NSW, lamb and chicken meat in Western Australia, and to a lesser degree, sugar in Queensland, and dairy products in a number of States).

Most of the reviews that have not yet passed to a policy stage affect small businesses, making reform politically difficult. Such reviews include a number of agricultural marketing arrangements, retail trading arrangements (including liquor licensing), taxi licensing, the regulation of the professions (including retail pharmacy arrangements) and mandatory insurance arrangements (such as workers' compensation and transport accident insurance). In a number of cases, such as for some agricultural marketing arrangements and for pharmacies,[76] reform is pending the development of policy at the national level.

Even though many of these reforms are likely to encounter strong resistance from the special interest groups that earn rents (at the expense of the rest of the community) from the restrictions on competition, it is nevertheless important that progress be made in these areas. Such reform will preserve the overall coherence of the NCP, contributing to a more efficient and dynamic economy. An important aspect of countering this pressure is for governments to step up efforts to explain to the community how NCP reforms contribute to higher living standards. Both the NCC and the Productivity Commission are active in this regard. In addition, there have been efforts to explain that changes in the economy reflect many influences other than the NCP. In particular, efforts have been made to explain to the rural community that their economic problems mainly stem from developments in the global economy, not the NCP, as some wrongly believe. In certain cases, structural adjustment assistance may be implemented. Even though reforms make the community better off, the rents that some individuals lose are likely to exceed their share of the gains in community prosperity. Adjustment assistance enables those resources released from effective competition to be deployed more rapidly to more productive uses. This includes consideration of the social costs of dislocation. If the reforms are worth implementing, there will still be a net gain to the community after paying compensation. This was the approach taken by the Northern Territory to liberalising taxi licenses – the government bought them back. Another approach is to phase reforms, allowing capital in the affected business to be rundown. This approach is likely to be most suited to situations where human and physical capital could not easily be redeployed. The approach that is preferable is likely to depend on the circumstances of each reform.

An area that has not yet been reviewed to the NCC's satisfaction is the Commonwealth Government's health care legislation. The restrictions on competition in this domain that most concern the NCC are the:

– introduction of limits on Medicare provider numbers in 1996;
– retention of numeric limits on Medicare eligible pathology centres; and
– impediments to competition in the private health insurance industry.

The Commonwealth Government retains the numeric restrictions to constrain growth in Medicare expenditure while the impediments to competition in private health insurance are to support community rating. The NCC does not consider that the Commonwealth Government has yet demonstrated that these restrictions on competition are in the public interest (including that the social objectives being pursued cannot be achieved in any other way).

Extension of competitive conduct laws

All jurisdictions have now enacted the co-operative legislative scheme which utilises Commonwealth and State constitutional power to extend the pro-competitive market rules of the *Trade Practices Act* 1973 to all businesses in Australia including, notably, State GBEs. These rules prohibit certain market fixing activities, such as price collusion between competing firms or large companies deliberately using their market power to damage competitors. Merger activity of large firms is also regulated by these rules. Prior to this reform, the competitive conduct rules applied only within the constitutional competence of the Commonwealth Government and thus, broadly, only applied to corporations, Commonwealth GBEs, and business transactions involving inter-State trade.

Tax reform

As in many other countries, the tax system in Australia has developed in an *ad hoc* way. It now has many features that conflict with principles of good taxation. Revenue security is undermined by excessive reliance on tax bases in long-term decline, such as the wholesale sales tax. There are many different indirect taxes with widely varying rates, which is likely to increase the dead-weight costs (excess burden) of raising any given amount of revenue. Marginal effective tax rates are high for many low-income persons, creating poverty traps. The highest marginal income tax rates come into effect at relatively modest income levels, raising concerns about equity and work and savings incentives. And vertical fiscal imbalance between the Commonwealth and States is growing over time because the Commonwealth has the main tax bases linked to economic activity. These problems, and the government's August 1998 tax package intended to address them were discussed in the 1999 OECD *Economic Survey of Australia*. The main features of this tax package were:

- the introduction of a 10 per cent Goods and Services Tax (GST) that would apply to the consumption of most goods and services, including imports;
- the abolition of the Wholesale Sales Tax;
- States to receive all revenue from the GST as compensation for the abrogation of the present Commonwealth General Financial Assistance Grants to States, conditional on the abolition of a range of narrowly based State indirect taxes identified as being highly inefficient;
- changing income tax brackets and rates so that marginal income tax rates decline for most persons;
- reductions in rates of benefit withdrawal to alleviate poverty traps; and
- compensation for persons on social security benefits and also for the self-supporting elderly.

This tax package was estimated to reduce the budget surpluses of the Commonwealth and the States in FY 2000-01 by A$ 4.8 billion (0.7 per cent of GDP) and A$ 0.7 billion (0.1 per cent of GDP), respectively. Taking both levels of government together, the package would have increased indirect taxes by a little more than the reduction in indirect taxes, with this revenue gain being more than offset by higher outlays.

Table 16. **Budget cost of modifications to the tax package**[1, 2]

A$ million

	2000-01	2001-02	2002-03
Extra expenditure (negative denotes increase in expenditure)			
Additional compensation package	730	540	870
Environmental package (expenditure)	213	223	227
Other expenditure	135	135	135
Total expenditure	1 078	898	1 232
Losses of revenue			
GST – basic food GST-free	3 090	3 640	3 860
GST – other	143	156	178
Total GST Package	3 233	3 796	4 038
Environment Package (revenue)	16	24	16
Total revenue	3 249	3 820	4 054
Total cost to government	4 327	4 718	5 286
Funding measures			
Additional revenue			
Income tax – reduced tax cuts	1 110	1 170	1 330
Diesel fuel excise and reduced credits	680	694	714
FID – defer abolition 6 months	523	109	0
Other state taxes – defer abolition[3]	568	2 217	2 420
Total funding measures	2 881	4 190	4 464
Net cost	1 446	528	822

1. The Commonwealth will retain funding responsibility for local government and will maintain funding guarantee arrangements. This will transfer expenditure from the States and Territories to the Commonwealth compared to that announced in A New Tax System and agreed by the States and Territories on 9 April 1999.
2. Costing compared to the 1999-2000 Budget estimates.
3. Excepting accommodation taxes and stamp duties on marketable securities which will be abolished according to the original schedule. Debits tax will be abolished by 1 July 2005.
Source: Commonwealth Treasury of Australia.

The package had to be modified to get the Senate's approval (the government does not have a majority in the Senate). The main changes were the exemption of basic food items from GST, reduced income tax cuts for persons earning more than A$ 50 000 per year,[77] the deferral of the abolition of certain State indirect taxes[78] and the provision of additional compensation for many social security beneficiaries (Table 16). In all, the changes increase the fiscal cost of the package by A$ 1.4 billion in FY 2000-01 but by significantly smaller amounts in subsequent years. The declining fiscal cost of the changes reflects the fact that the savings from deferring the abolition of various State indirect taxes is only relevant in subsequent years, when they were originally scheduled to be abolished. In all, the revised package will reduce government surpluses by A$ 6.9 billion (1.0 per cent of GDP) in FY 2000-01 and by a similar amount as a share of GDP in FY 2002-03 (Table 17). There is still a shift from direct to indirect taxes, although it is less marked than in the original package. The modifications to the tax

Table 17. **Budget impact of the final tax package**[1]

A$ billion

	1999-2000	2000-01	2001-02	2002-03
Direct tax				
Personal	0.72	−10.58	−10.69	−11.45
Business	0.12	1.67	0.97	0.65
Administration	0.16	1.66	3.97	2.8
Indirect tax				
GST revenue	0.00	23.97	28.16	28.77
Taxes abolished/reduced	0.00	−7.10	−10.05	−10.34
Other	−0.31	−8.71	−10.84	−11.71
Other	0.00	1.03	0.83	0.97
Total revenue	0.68	1.94	2.35	−0.31
Total outlays	−1.90	−8.83	−6.99	−7.76
Total impact	−1.22	−6.89	−4.64	−8.07
(per cent of GDP)	−0.2	−1.0	−0.7	−1.1

1. Relative to budget projections in the absence of tax reform. The projection in this table have been made by adding together those in the Government's original tax package and the projected additional costs of the tax package as finally agreed with the senate and announced by the Prime Minister.
Source: Commonwealth Treasury (1998), "Tax Reform – Not a New Tax – A New Tax System"; Prime Minister's Press Release of 28 May 1999 on the New Tax Package; and OECD Secretariat.

package do not affect the inroads into the high marginal effective tax rates on low-income earners planned in the original tax package. By increasing tax free income thresholds for families (including sole parents) and lowering benefit withdrawal rates, the package will reduce the marginal effective tax rates for low income working families from 85.5 per cent to 61.5 per cent over a substantial range of income. Moreover, as the proposed personal income tax cuts on incomes below A$ 50 000 remain intact, it is still true that the tax package will result in some 80 per cent of taxpayers having marginal income tax rates of 30 per cent or lower. Nevertheless, the delay in abolishing various harmful State indirect taxes, especially the tax on bank account debits, is unfortunate as it waters down the gains from reform.

The next item on the government's tax reform agenda is business taxation. The main problem with existing arrangements is the inconsistent treatment of business entities and the investment they conduct, with large and variable gaps between tax treatment and commercial reality. In *A New Tax System* (*Commonwealth Treasury*, 1998), the government proposed to address these issues by:

- applying a framework of redesigned company taxation arrangements consistently to all limited liability entities; and
- possibly, by considering the favourable tax treatment (including accelerated depreciation) for certain forms of business investment.

The extra revenue from these base-broadening measures would be available to finance a reduction in the company tax rate and to provide relief from capital gains tax.

The Committee appointed under the Chairmanship of Mr Ralph to consult interested parties on the broad lines of business tax reform outlined in A *New Tax System* and to make recommendations on such reforms has reported to the government and it has announced its response. This is in two stages, with a phased implementation. First stage measures include:

– *lowering the company tax rate* from 36 per cent to 34 per cent for the 2000-01 income tax year and to 30 per cent thereafter. The counterpart to this is the abolition of accelerated depreciation (but consideration is to be given to providing investment allowances for strategic investments);
– *lowering the effective capital gains tax rate* by subjecting only 50 per cent of individuals' capital gains and 67 per cent of superannuation funds' capital gains to taxation. However, indexation and averaging arrangements for assessing capital gains are to be removed. Capital gains taxation for small businesses is to be reduced further and there will be rollover relief for scrip-for-scrip takeovers between companies and between fixed trusts. In addition, investments by non-resident tax exempt pension funds and certain investments by superannuation funds in venture capital investments are to be exempt from capital gains tax.
– *reducing the compliance burden for small businesses* (defined as businesses with an annual turnover of less than A$ 1 million).

Second stage measures will include the Government's response to recommendations to:

– improve integrity measures, including in respect of the alienation of personal services income;
– provide imputation credits for foreign dividend withholding tax up to 15 per cent;
– improve policy, legislation and administrative practices;
– replace the existing law based on legal definitions of income with a more structured framework for the treatment of expenditure and assets.

The first and second stage measures are intended to be broadly revenue neutral over the period of the forward estimates. The first package of business tax legislation has been introduced into the Parliament. Further packages are expected to be introduced later this year and early next year.

Notes

1. Fiscal years begin 1 July.

2. Accordingly referred to by some observers as the "miracle economy".

3. This applies to both final and total domestic demand, with no unusual contribution of stock building to GDP growth in fiscal years 1997-98 to 1998-99. The non-farm inventories-to-sales ratio appears to have fallen below desired levels in 1997-98, reflecting unexpectedly strong sales over that period. The increase in non-farm inventories in the first half of 1999 is likely to have returned non-farm stockholding more in line with requirements, although there was probably some unexpected stockbuilding in the manufacturing sector due to weaker than expected sales. The conspicuous strong growth contribution of inventories in calendar year 1998 is largely a rebound effect of the rundown in total inventories in 1997. The latter is explained by the treatment of gold sales by the Reserve Bank of Australia and the export of a frigate to New Zealand in the national accounts, both of which led to a reduction in public authority stocks when the exports came into effect.

4. The series is by nature very volatile and subject to revision: on a seasonally-adjusted basis, the household saving ratio was at around 1½ per cent in the first three quarters of FY 1998-99, but jumped to slightly above 3 per cent in the June quarter.

5. The household saving ratio shown in Figure 4 is a net measure, that is, consumption of fixed capital has been deducted from the measure of income. Since depreciation has generally accounted for a rising proportion of gross saving, net saving measures have declined by more than gross measures.

6. A notable example is the partial privatisation of the telecommunications company Telstra in late 1997, which turned out to be very profitable for subscribers and is likely to have had a stimulating effect on household spending.

7. An outstanding example of the latter is the demutualisation of the Australian Mutual Provident Fund (AMP), the largest Australian insurance company in 1998. Although the demutualisation did not create wealth, it made it easily accessible and transferable.

8. The Melbourne Institute's Survey of Consumer Sentiment.

9. The private sector's purchase of a natural gas pipeline from the public enterprise sector resulted in the striking rise of the private business sector investment in buildings and structures, and as counterpart the steep decline in public enterprises' investment shown in Table 1 for the first half of 1998.

10. This has also been boosted by privatisations and the ongoing trend towards incorporatisation of businesses.

11. However, the trade surplus in the first half of 1997 was generated by two special factors: gold sales of the Reserve Bank (A\$ 1.8 billion) and the sale of a frigate to New

Zealand (A$ 0.5 billion). Hence, adjusted for these one-off factors, the trade account would just have been in balance.

12. The market sector excludes sectors in which outputs are not valued in the market. The sectors excluded are: property and business services; government administration and defence; education; health and community services; and personal and other services, including ownership of dwellings. The market sector covered 62 per cent of GDP in 1997-98. Hourly labour productivity growth for the total economy was somewhat lower than in the market sector: 3 per cent in 1998 and 2¼ per cent (annualised) in the first half of 1999.

13. See Bernie, K. and P. Downes (1999). However, the 95 per cent confidence interval on this point estimate ranges from 4 to 8¾ per cent.

14. Until the September quarter of 1998, the CPI was constructed on the basis of the "outlays" approach, which implied the inclusion of mortgage interest charges in the CPI as a measure of the cost of owner-occupied housing. This had the perverse effect that a rise in policy interest rates to reduce anticipated inflation pressures, regularly raised the rate of CPI inflation in the short run. To avoid this consequence, the Reserve Bank focussed on the Treasury underlying inflation rate for the formulation and evaluation of monetary policy. The ABS' new "acquisitions" approach to the CPI measures the cost of acquiring a new dwelling (excluding land) rather than the outlays involved in servicing the mortgage which financed the purchase, which avoids the noted perverse interest effect on the inflation measure. Differences between the new ("headline") CPI and the Treasury underlying measure of inflation reflect the exclusion of volatile items or other special factors from the underlying measure. Following the move from an outlays to an acquisitions approach to measuring consumer prices, the inflation target is now expressed in terms of the new "headline" CPI. For more details see "The Implications of Recent Changes to the Consumer Price Index for Monetary Policy and the Inflation Target", Reserve Bank of Australia *Bulletin*, October 1998.

15. Conducted by the Australian Centre for Industrial Relations Research and Training (ACIRRT).

16. The WCI has been developed by the ABS to provide a more accurate indicator of changes in wage rates than current measures available in the Average Weekly Earnings Survey and the national accounts' surveys. The WCI measures changes in the wage cost of a representative sample of employee jobs (for a fixed "basket" of jobs). It is a 'pure price' index reflecting changes in hourly rates of pay resulting from a range of sources including award variations, enterprise and workplace agreements, centralised wage fixing, individual contracts, and informal agreements.

17. The projections embody information available at 3 November 1999.

18. The Reserve Bank first indicated an informal inflation target in 1993. A clear and transparent Statement on the Conduct of Monetary Policy was agreed between the Treasurer and the Reserve Bank Governor in August 1996, which formalised the medium-term targeting approach. The Statement also underlined the independence of the Reserve Bank in conducting monetary policy. See also the 1997 OECD Economic Survey of Australia, Chapter II.

19. Until the September quarter of 1998, the inflation target referred to the Commonwealth Treasury measure of underlying inflation. Following changes to the construction of the CPI, including the removal of mortgage interest charges from the index, the

RBA's inflation target is defined in terms of the total CPI since the December quarter of 1998.

20. Actually, a small budget surplus was achieved in 1997-98 in terms of the former cash underlying balance measure, which was targeted by the Commonwealth Government until FY 1998-99. This measure excludes "net advances", which consist primarily of asset sales and net repayments of debt by the states to the Commonwealth.

21. The cash rate is the overnight money market interest rate which the RBA controls through open-market operations with a high degree of precision.

22. M3 is defined as currency plus bank deposits of the private non-bank sector. Broad money comprises M3 plus borrowings from the private sector by non-bank financial institutions, less the latter's holdings of currency and bank deposits.

23. OECD estimate, using average export and import weights and covering 42 countries.

24. Defined as the ratio of the National Accounts deflators of exports to imports of goods and services.

25. The MCI used for the analysis is defined as $MCI = (r - r^*) + 0.31(e/e^* - 1) - 7(t/t^* - 1)$, where r is the real 90-day bill yield (using the Treasury underlying rate of inflation as deflator), r^* the long-term trend value of r, e the real effective exchange rate expressed as relative unit labour cost in common currency, e^* the long-term trend value of e, t the terms of trade as ratio of implicit deflators of exports and imports of goods and services, and t^* the long-term trend of t. In addition to real interest rate and real exchange rate indicators, the MCI used here also incorporates a terms-of-trade variable. This takes account of the observation that swings in the real effective exchange rate of the Australian dollar are often driven by changes in the terms of trade, which have effects on demand opposite to those of movements in the real exchange rate. As long-term trend values for r, e and t the non-stationary component of a Hodrick-Prescott filter has been used, with a smoothing factor of 1 600. The weights on the exchange rate and terms of trade variables are based on model simulations. A positive MCI implies tight monetary conditions relative to long-term averages.

26. The simulation exercise has been simplified by using as real MCI the sum of the change in the real short-term interest rate and the real exchange rate, with a weight of 0.3 on the latter variable. The implicit private consumption deflator has been used as deflator.

27. These principles include: achieving adequate national saving; moderating cyclical fluctuations; maintaining Commonwealth net debt at prudent levels; pursuing spending and taxing policies that are consistent with a reasonable degree of stability and predictability in the tax burden; maintaining the integrity of the tax system; and ensuring that policy decisions have regard to their financial effects on future generations.

28. By contrast, net debt only takes into account financial assets.

29. On a cash basis.

30. This estimate was provided in Commonwealth Treasury (1998), *Tax Reform – Not a New Tax – A New System* and was reproduced in OECD (1999), *Economic Survey of Australia*, Table 18.

31. These payments amount to about A$ 1¼ billion in FY 1998-99 and subsequent years. Previously, these payments were made below the budget line.

32. The estimates and projections in this section come from government budgets unless otherwise stated.

33. These initiatives added about 0.8 per cent of GDP to outlays. Including these payments, the underlying balance fell as a share of GDP from a surplus of 0.3 per cent in FY 1997-98 to a deficit of 0.6 per cent in FY 1998-99.

34. It is assumed for these estimates that the trend rate of economic growth equals the long-term average, $3^1/_2$ per cent; the Commonwealth Treasury estimates the potential growth rate to be $3^1/_2$ to 4 per cent. The semi-elasticity of net-lending as a percentage of GDP with respect to cyclical growth is estimated to be 0.37 (OECD, forthcoming).

35. Data on debt in this section refer to the position on 30 June of the year indicated, expressed as a percentage of GDP in the fiscal year ending on 30 June. For example, debt in 1995 refers to debt as at 30 June 1995 expressed as a percentage of GDP in 1994-95.

36. Net debt excludes trade debits and credits, in contrast to net liabilities. For comparison, general government net liabilities were 28 per cent of GDP in 1995 and 17 per cent in 1998.

37. Since the draft was finalised and approved by the Committee, changes to the national accounts have led to an upward revision to the flow of capital services from the capital stock and hence some downward revision in estimates of the growth of total factor productivity (TFP). These revisions have affected all periods going back to the 1960s. The increase in TFP growth in the 1990s is of a broadly similar magnitude but starts from a lower base.

38. For a definition see footnote 12 above.

39. The Australian Bureau of Statistics (ABS) determines productivity cycles. It calculates a trend productivity series (using a Henderson 11-period moving average) and identifies productivity peaks in years in which the gap between the actual and trend productivity series turns from increasing to decreasing.

40. The Productivity Commission calculates that 0.4 percentage point of this 2.4 per cent TFP growth rate is attributable to industry composition effects.

41. The experience following the earlier period of high TFP growth suggests that caution is in order when assessing future trends. The four-year average annual rate of TFP growth also exceeded 2 per cent for three years running (1969-70 to 1971-72) in the earlier period, even though the rate for the productivity cycle (1968-69 to 1973-74) was only 1.6 per cent. Historically, there have been large swings in TFP growth (see Figure 22).

42. Other things equal, a higher capital-labour ratio reduces capital productivity (and increases labour productivity) owing to diminishing returns.

43. Trend data have been by obtained by applying a Hodrick-Prescott (100) filter to the actual data.

44. In Australia, industrial awards generally specify minimum wages and conditions of work for most categories of labour. It is, thus, illegal to employ a worker at a wage or on terms which are less favourable than the relevant award, irrespective of whether a worker is a union member or not. The terms of awards may be reached by a settlement imposed by the Australian Industrial Relations Commission or similar industrial tribunals by the states, by a combination of conciliation and arbitration, or by conciliation alone.

45. For more details on the coverage of the "allowable matters" see footnote 35 of last year's OECD Economic Survey of Australia.

46. Certified agreements which enable individual firms and trade unions to negotiate wages and conditions of work were already introduced by the Industrial Relations Act 1988, which was amended in 1992. The "non-union" certified agreements are designed to promote enterprise bargaining between employees and their firms in lightly or "non-unionised" workplaces.

47. These agreements are required to be certified by the AIRC, subject to the "no-disadvantage test", which stipulates that any new collective or individual agreement must make sure that workers entering them would not be worse off as a result. However, unlike the narrower "no-disadvantage test" which was in force before 1997, the current "global" version of the test allows award entitlements to be traded off – under certain conditions – as long as a new enterprise agreement is in general terms no less favourable to the employee than the relevant award or relevant law. See also Chapter III of the 1999 OECD Economic Survey of Australia.

48. The Employment Advocate is a new statutory office established under the WRA. The tasks of the Employment Advocate are to make sure that the nature of a workplace agreement is sufficiently explained to a concerned employee, that the employee genuinely consents to the making of the agreement and that the workplace agreement meets the "no-disadvantage test".

49. To put these figures into perspective, it should be noted that about one-third of the employees work on the basis of informal arrangements or individual contracts outside the award and enterprise agreement system.

50. For empirical support for the positive correlation between a widening wage dispersion and private sector employment growth see Chapter 5 of the OECD Jobs Study (1994), Part II.

51. See Norris, K. and B. McLean (1999),

52. Success in getting marginal workers from unemployment into lower paid jobs also increases the earnings dispersion, but would seem a desirable outcome.

53. Data for the second half of the 1990s are not available yet.

54. Defined as the proportion of individuals falling below one half of median equivalent household disposable income. Equivalent household disposable income is the income of all members of a household divided by the square root of the number of individuals in the household (see Oxley et al., 1997, Box B). Child poverty, however, in spite of its significant reduction during the ten years ending in the mid-1990s, remained somewhat above the OECD average, probably reflecting a relatively high share of children living in lone-parent and non-working households.

55. The federal system has always been the sole system in the Northern Territory and the Capital Territory, while since the beginning of 1997, Victoria's system has been integrated in the federal system through a referral of powers by the Victorian government.

56. For more details see Chapter III of last year's OECD Economic Survey of Australia.

57. However, although the more effective compliance provisions introduced by the WRA undoubtedly helped to cut back the number of labour disputes in 1997-98, the downward trend in the number of working days lost by industrial action had begun already in the early 1980s, probably also reflecting the "accord policy" from 1983 to 1995.

58. On the basis of a number of indicators for the period 1985 to 1993, the OECD *Jobs Study*, Part II (1994), concluded that Australia's overall employment protection legislation was among the least strict in the OECD. Indeed, a ranking of OECD countries placed Australia fourth out of 21 countries: only the United States, New Zealand and Canada were found to have had less restrictive employment protection legislation (*ibid*, Table 6.7, Panel B, column 2). However, changes in unfair dismissal provisions in the 1993 Industrial Relations Reform Act are likely to have moved Australia's employment protection legislation into the direction of greater strictness. In response to the surge in unfair dismissal cases lodged after the Act had come into effect, and to employer complaints over disincentives to hiring, the unfair dismissal legislation was amended in 1994, and again in 1996. The aim of the latest amendment is to minimise legal costs and discourage frivolous and malicious claims, *inter alia* through the requirement of a filing fee, the ability of the AIRC to arbitrate rather than the claim going to court, and the increased emphasis on the substantive reasons for dismissal rather than procedural aspects. However, these changes appear to have done too little to limit the overall cost involved in terminating an employee, especially for smaller firms.

59. As opposed to the more radical approach, adopted by New Zealand in 1991, which abolished industry-wide awards and replaced them with a system of free contracting of employees and employers.

60. See Sloan's (1998) critical assessment of the result of the simplification of the Hospitality Industry Award in late 1997, which was a test case of award simplification. Sloan judges the pruning of 22 matters from the original Hospitality Industry Award as "mainly trivial, with some exceptions".

61. See Commonwealth Department of Employment, Education, Training and Youth Affairs of Australia (1994). For a brief overview of major elements of the Working Nation programme see the 1995 OECD Economic of Survey of Australia, Chapter III.

62. See Commonwealth Department of Employment, Education, Training and Youth Affairs (1996).

63. Brokered programmes are contracted out to various organisations – the brokers – and provide participants with both training and work experience for at least six months. In effect, they are mainly job creation projects with some training provided. For more details see the 1996 OECD *Economic Survey of Australia*, Annex I.

64. Unlike in most other OECD countries which have unemployment insurance systems, Australia's unemployment benefits are in the nature of social assistance: they are means-tested, of indefinite duration and dependent on family circumstances. The condition for unemployment benefit eligibility is that claimants must be available for full-time work, actively seeking it and willing to accept any suitable job offer they receive.

65. Youth Allowance was introduced on 1 July 1998. It has replaced the Newstart Allowance for people aged 18 to 20 who are looking for work. Unlike the Newstart Allowance, the amount of Youth Allowance that an individual is entitled to depends on a parental means test.

66. Apart from Work for the Dole projects, these activities cover a wide range of other community development projects as well as training courses, such as literacy and numeracy training, apprenticeship programmes, job search and placement instructions, and career counselling.

67. See Commonwealth Department of Employment, Workplace Relations and Small Business (1999). The report is available on the Internet: http://www.dewrsb.gov.au/group_lmp/files/work_for_dole_evaluation/evaluation_of_work_for_the_dole.htm

68. "Document literacy" refers to the knowledge and skills required to locate and use information contained in various formats such as job applications, payroll forms, transportation timetables, maps tables and diagrams. The other dimensions of literacy that have been surveyed in the IALS are: "prose literacy", which refers to the knowledge and skills required to use and understand information from texts; and "quantitative literacy", which refers to the skills and knowledge required to apply arithmetic operations to numbers embedded in printed materials. Australia did not participate in the surveys on prose literacy and quantitative literacy.

69. This obligation is set out in clause 4 of the Competition Principles Agreement.

70. In relation to the sale of TasRail, the government is considering the extent to which the issues raised by clause 4 have been otherwise considered and whether the intent of clause 4 has been fulfilled (National Competition Council, 1999c).

71. National Competition Council (1999b).

72. A case in point is the construction of an interconnection pipeline between the Victorian and NSW gas systems. This pipeline has also enhanced security of supply. The importance of this aspect was highlighted in 1998 when increased supplies of gas flowed from NSW following the accident that shut off Victoria's own supplies.

73. Currently, competition is only permitted for mail weighing more than 250 grams or where the delivery fee exceeds A$ 1.80 (i.e. four times the standard letter rate).

74. For example, in NSW 72 licence schemes have been repealed and 13 others are to be repealed (National Competition Council, 1999c).

75. Reforms were made to the regulation of chiropractors and osteopaths in 1996, optometrists and chiropodists in 1997 and physiotherapists in 1998.

76. A national review is expected to commence in the second half of 1999.

77. The tax cuts for those earning over A$ 50 000 are to be reduced by increasing the proposed 40 per cent rate bracket (A$ 50 001-60 000) to 42 per cent and by reducing the proposed threshold for the top rate of 47 per cent from A$ 75 000 to A$ 60 000.

78. The abolition of Financial Institutions Duty (FID) is to be deferred by six months, to 1 July 2001. The time limit for abolishing the debits tax (on bank accounts) has been pushed back to 1 July 2005 and is subject to review by the Ministerial Council, comprising Commonwealth and State Treasurers, established under the Intergovernmental Agreement on the Reform of Commonwealth-State Financial Relations. The need for retention of the remaining business stamp duties will be reviewed by the Ministerial Council by 2005. These stamp duties apply to: non-residential conveyances; leases; mortgages, debentures, bonds and other loan securities; credit arrangements, instalment purchase arrangements and rental arrangements; cheques, bills of exchange and promissory notes and unquoted marketable securities. Accommodation taxes and stamp duty on marketable securities are to be abolished from 1 July 2000 and 1 July 2001, respectively, as provided for in the original tax package.

Bibliography

Ainley, John (1998),
"School Participation, Retention and Outcomes", in Dusseldorp Skills Forum (1998), *Australia's Youth: Reality and Risk.*

Ainley, John and Phil McKenzie (1999),
"The influence of school factors", in Dusseldorp Skills Forum (1999), *Australia's Young Adults: The Deepening Divide.*

Australian Bureau of Statistics (1999),
Schools Australia 1998, Catalogue No. 4221.0, Canberra.

Bernie, K. and P. Downes (1999),
"The Macroeconomics of Unemployment in the Treasury Macroeconomic (TRYM) Model", paper presented at the Reserve Bank of Australia, *Seminar Series*, January.

Commonwealth Department of Employment, Education, Training and Youth Affairs (1994), *Working Nation, Policies and Programs*, AGPS, Canberra.

Commonwealth Department of Employment, Education, Training and Youth Affairs (1996), *Working Nation: Evaluation of the Employment, Education and Training Elements*, EMB Report 2/96, AGPS, Canberra.

Commonwealth Department of Employment, Workplace Relations and Small Business (1999),
Evaluation of the Work for the Dole Pilot Programme, EMB Report 1/99, AusInfo, Canberra.

Commonwealth Treasury (1998),
Tax Reform- Not a New Tax- A New System, Overview, AGPS, Canberra.

Dusseldorp Skills Forum (1997),
School-Industry Programs: Some Comparisons Between the States and the Territories.

Dusseldorp Skills Forum (1998),
Australia's Youth: Reality and Risk.

Dusseldorp Skills Forum (1999),
Australia's Young Adults: The Deepening Divide.

Gruen, D., A. Pagan and C. Thompson (1999),
"The Phillips Curve in Australia", *Research Discussion Paper* 1999-01, Reserve Bank of Australia, January.

Klerman, J. and L. Karoly (1995),
"The Transition to Stable Employment: The Experience of US Youth in Their Early Labor Market Career", National Center for Research in Vocational Education, Berkeley, CA.

Maglen, Leo and Chandra Shah (1999),
"Emerging Occupational Patterns in Australia in the era of Globalisation and Rapid

Technological Change: Implications for Education and Training", Monash University – ACER Centre for the Economics of Education and Training.

Marks, Gary N. and Nicole Fleming (1999),
"Early School Leaving in Australia: Findings from the 1995 Year 9 LSAY Cohort", Longitudinal Surveys of Australian Youth Research Report Number 11, Australian Council for Educational Research.

McClelland, Alison and MacDonald (1999),
"Young Adults and Labour Market Disadvantage?", in Dusseldorp Skills Forum (1999), Australia's Young Adults: The Deepening Divide.

National Competition Council (1999a),
National Competition Policy: Some Impacts on Society and the Economy.

National Competition Council (1999b),
Annual Report 1998-99.

National Competition Council (1999c),
National Competition Policy Second Tranche Assessment.

Norris, K. and B. McLean (1999),
"Changes in Earnings Inequality, 1975 to 1998", Australian Bulletin of Labour, Vol. 25, March.

OECD,
Economic Surveys of Australia, Paris, various years.

OECD (1994),
The OECD Jobs Study, Evidence and Explanations, Part II: The Adjustment Potential of the Labour Market, Paris.

OECD (1998),
Education at a Glance: OECD Indicators.

Oxley, H., J.-M. Burniaux, T.-T. Dang and M. Mira d'Ercole (1997),
"Income Distribution and Poverty in 13 OECD Countries", OECD Economic Studies, No. 29.

Oxley, H., T.-T. Dang, M. Förster and M. Pellizzari (1999),
"Income Inequalities and Poverty Among Children and Households with Children in Selected OECD Countries: Trends and Determinants", unpublished manuscript.

Polesel, J. and R. Teese (1997),
VET in Schools: The Transition from School, University of Melbourne.

Productivity Commission (1999),
Progress in Rail Reform, Draft Report.

Reserve Bank of Australia (1998),
"The Implications of Recent Changes to the Consumer Price Index for Monetary Policy and the Inflation Target", Bulletin, October.

Schröeder, L. (1996),
"Dead End Jobs and Upgrading Plans: An evaluation of Job Creation Programmes", in Wadensjö, E. (ed.), The Nordic Labour Markets in the 1990s, Part 2, Elsevier, Amsterdam.

Senate Employment, Education and Training References Committee (Chair, R. Crowley) (1997),
A Class Act: Inquiry into the Status of the Teaching Profession, Canberra.

Sloan, J. (1998),
"The Australian Labour Market –; March 1998", *Australian Bulletin of Labour*, Vol. 24.

Spierings, John (1999),
"A Crucial Point in Life: Learning, Work and Young Adults", in Dusseldorp Skills Forum (1999), *Australia's Young Adults: The Deepening Divide.*

Sweet, Richard (1998),
"Youth: The Rhetoric and the Reality of the 1990s", in Dusseldorp Skills Forum (1998), *Australia's Youth: Reality and Risk.*

Victorian Government (1999),
Benefits of Reform, Victorian Office of Regulation Reform (http://www.dsd.vic.gov/regreform).

Werner, Mark and John, David (1999),
Australian Apprentice and Trainee Statistics, Trends 1995-1998. An Overview, National Centre for Vocational Education Research.

Annex I

Deriving the fiscal balance*

The fiscal balance can be derived from the operating result by making adjustments for revaluations and for capital. Revaluations are removed from the operating result because they do not affect the Government's resource position. Rather, they reflect changes in the values of assets and liabilities resulting from flows that are not transactions. Charges for capital use or depreciation are removed from the operating result and replaced with capital expenditure because the objective is to measure government's full investment net of saving in a period. These adjustments are summarised in Table A1 for the years covered by the Budget estimates and projections.

---

* This section is based on Commonwealth Treasury of Australia (1999), *Budget Strategy and Outlook 1999-2000*, Statement 1, Appendix A.

Table A1. **Deriving the fiscal balance**

	1998-99	1999-2000	2000-01	2001-02	2002-03
	Total estimate		Total projection		
1. **Underlying cash balance (new treatment)**	**2 883**	**5 208**	**3 114**	**7 210**	**12 460**
plus net advances	5 511	17 828	−923	17 658	16 698
Headline cash balance	8 394	23 036	2 190	24 867	29 159
less GFS/AAS31 classification differences	851	1 867	750	2 484	27
less net cash from investing activities	1 020	11 404	−5 199	10 930	11 826
plus accrual adjustments (revenues not providing cash plus cash used "provided" by working capital items less expenses not requiring cash)	−3 358	−4 049	80	−6 051	−5 674
Operating result	3 166	5 717	6 718	5 402	11 633
2. *plus* total accrual adjustments	283	509	3 604	−1 808	−827
3. **Operating result (before abnormals)**	**3 166**	**5 717**	**6 718**	**5 402**	**11 633**
4. *plus* revaluations/writedowns from superannuation	0	0	0	0	0
5. *plus* net writedown of assets/bad and doubtful debts	1 134	1 066	974	1 059	1 073
6. *plus* net foreign exchange losses	−500	2	2	2	2
7. *plus* other economic revaluations	810	386	693	331	33
8. *less* profit (loss) on the sale of assets	2	−34	−13	−22	−11
9. *less* costs of asset sales	60	224	0	218	218
10. **GFS operating result**	**4 548**	**6 981**	**8 401**	**6 597**	**12 533**
11. *less* purchase of property plant and equipment, and intangibles	4 579	4 989	4 838	5 055	4 967
12. *less* assets acquired under finance leases	n.a.	n.a.	n.a.	n.a.	n.a.
13. *less* other non-financial leases	123	9	−25	1	−3
14. *less* increase in inventories	−250	−156	−107	7	−62
15. *plus* proceeds from sales of property, plant and equipment and intangibles	701	810	725	699	553
16. *plus* depreciation and amortisation	2 308	2 477	2 776	2 956	3 169
17. **Fiscal balance (GFS net lending)**	**3 105**	**5 426**	**7 195**	**5 189**	**11 353**

1.   Items 4 to 9 reflect revaluations. Items 11 to 16 reflect the capital adjustment.
Source: Commonwealth Treasury of Australia, *Budget Strategy and Outlook*, 1999-2000.

Annex II

Sector contributions to the actual increase in productivity growth*

The sectors that most improved their labour productivity growth in the latest productivity cycle are: wholesale trade; electricity, gas and water supply (EGW); mining; finance and insurance; and construction (Table A2). All of these sectors except EGW and mining also raised their capital productivity growth by more than the average. The increases in labour productivity growth in EGW and in mining were associated with an increased rate of capital deepening, contributing to a relative decline in capital productivity growth. In addition to the sectors identified as having above average increases in the growth of both labour- and capital productivity, transport and storage also recorded an above average increase in total factor productivity growth. But productivity growth in all of these sectors except construction was very low relative to trend in the previous productivity cycle. Accordingly, the large increase in productivity growth in the latest productivity cycle may to some represent a correction to the poor performance in the previous productivity cycle. A better indication of the sectors that have most contributed to improved productivity growth can be obtained by analysing trend data.

---

* Based on actual, as opposed to trend, data.

Table A2. Productivity growth, by sector[1]

	Constant price weight[3,4]	Labour productivity growth			Capital productivity growth			Total factor productivity[2]			Capital-labour ratio growth		
		1988-89 to 1993-94	1993-94 to 1997-98	Change	1988-89 to 1993-94	1993-94 to 1997-98	Change	1988-89 to 1993-94	1993-94 to 1997-98	Change	1988-89 to 1993-94	1993-94 to 1997-98	Change
A. Agriculture, forestry and fishing	5.3	5.6	-1.9	-7.5	2.4	0.4	-2.1	4.0	-0.9	-4.9	3.2	-2.3	-5.4
B. Mining	7.5	5.3	7.6	2.3	0.6	0.6	0.0	2.0	2.8	0.7	4.7	7.0	2.3
C. Manufacturing	20.8	4.2	1.9	-2.3	-1.0	-1.1	-0.1	2.4	0.8	-1.6	5.3	3.0	-2.3
D. Electricity, gas and water supply	4.5	7.3	10.7	3.4	5.2	-3.2	-8.4	5.9	0.6	-5.2	2.1	13.9	11.8
E. **Construction**	9.5	0.6	2.8	**2.2**	-2.3	1.7	**4.0**	0.0	2.5	**2.5**	3.0	1.1	-1.8
F. **Wholesale trade**	9.7	-1.4	8.2	**9.7**	-0.7	4.3	**5.0**	-1.2	7.0	**8.2**	-0.8	4.0	4.7
G. Retail trade	9.7	1.8	1.9	0.1	-1.2	-1.5	-0.2	1.1	1.1	0.0	3.1	3.4	0.3
H. Accommodation, cafes and restaurants	3.6	-1.0	-0.5	0.6	-2.8	-4.6	-1.8	-1.5	-1.4	0.1	1.8	4.2	2.4
I. **Transport and storage**	10.6	1.7	2.0	0.3	-1.9	2.0	**3.9**	0.3	2.0	**1.7**	3.7	0.0	-3.7
I. Communication services	4.9	9.5	6.7	-2.8	-4.6	0.3	**4.8**	2.3	3.4	1.1	14.1	6.5	-7.6
K. **Finance and insurance**	10.2	3.5	5.8	**2.3**	-1.7	2.6	**4.3**	1.2	4.2	**3.1**	5.2	3.2	-2.0
P. Cultural and recreational services	3.1	-0.5	0.5	1.0	-1.8	-3.8	-1.9	-1.0	-1.0	0.0	1.4	4.3	2.9
Market sector	100.0	2.0	3.2	1.2	-0.7	0.8	1.5	1.1	2.4	1.2	2.8	2.4	-0.4

1. The sectors with the largest changes in total factor productivity growth are highlighted in the first column. The largest changes in each category of productivity growth are shown by bolding the figures in the relevant column.
2. Calculated using a Tornqvist index.
3. At basic prices, 1997-98.
4. Reference year for chain volume measures is 1996-97.
Source: Australian Bureau of Statistics and OECD Secretariat.

Annex III

Second tranche national competition policy non-compliance issues and recommendations

Table A3. **Second tranche non-compliance issues and recommendations on 1999-2000 competition payments**

	Second tranche non-compliance issues	Recommendations on competition payments
Commonwealth	– No review of structural and regulatory arrangements prior to privatising Australian National (see section B4.2). – No review of structural and regulatory arrangements prior to privatising the Tasmanian rail services (TasRail) (see section B4.2).	– Not applicable.
New South Wales	– Nil; subject to outstanding second tranche issues in Table A4.	– Full payment of first part of second tranche NCP payments due in 1999-2000. – Second tranche NCP payments due in 2000-01 subject to supplementary assessment of identified outstanding second tranche issues (see Table A4).
Victoria	– Nil; subject to outstanding second tranche issues in Table A4.	– Full payment of first part of second tranche NCP payments due in 1999-2000. – Second tranche NCP payments due in 2000-01 subject to supplementary assessment of identified outstanding second tranche issues (see Table A4).
Queensland	– Demonstration of robust independent appraisals being conducted to determine economic viability and ecological sustainability prior to investment in rural schemes and/or implementation of the recommendations of such appraisals (see section B10.4.2).	– Suspension of 25 per cent of second tranche 1999-2000 competition payments until 31 December 1999. Final recommendation on these payments to be made by 31 December 1999 following a supplementary assessment. – Second tranche NCP payments due in 2000-01 subject to supplementary assessment of identified outstanding second tranche issues (see Table A4).
Western Australia	– Nil; subject to outstanding second tranche issues in Table A4.	– Full payment of first part of second tranche NCP payments due in 1999-2000. – Second tranche NCP payments due in 2000-01 subject to supplementary assessment of identified outstanding second tranche issues (see Table A4).

Table A3. **Second tranche non-compliance issues and recommendations on 1999-2000 competition payments** *(cont.)*

	Second tranche non-compliance issues	Recommendations on competition payments
South Australia	– Nil; subject to outstanding second tranche issues in Table A4.	– Full payment of first part of second tranche NCP payments due in 1999-2000.
		– Second tranche NCP payments due in 2000-01 subject to supplementary assessment of identified outstanding second tranche issues (see Table A4).
Tasmania	– Nil; subject to outstanding second tranche issues in Table A4.	– Full payment of first part of second tranche NCP payments due in 1999-2000.
		– Second tranche NCP payments due in 2000-01 subject to supplementary assessment of identified outstanding second tranche issues (see Table A4).
Australian Capital Territory	– Nil; subject to outstanding second tranche issues in Table A4.	– Full payment of first part of second tranche NCP payments due in 1999-2000.
		– Second tranche NCP payments due in 2000-01 subject to supplementary assessment of identified outstanding second tranche issues (see Table A4).
Northern Territory	– Nil; subject to outstanding second tranche issues in Table A4.	– Full payment of first part of second tranche NCP payments due in 1999-2000.
		– Second tranche NCP payments due in 2000-01 subject to supplementary assessment of identified outstanding second tranche issues (see Table A4).

Source: National Competition Council (1999c).

Table A4. **Second tranche issues subject to supplementary assessment**

Second tranche issues	Comment
Commonwealth	
– Establishment of an effective access regime to Australia Post's network to enhance competition in line with review recommendations (see section B5.4.8).	– Compliance with NCP depends on adoption of an acceptable access regime. The Council is to examine progress on this matter in subsequent assessments.
– Incomplete implementation of road transport reforms (see section B9.4): • Reform 2: Uniform or consistent national registration requirements for heavy vehicles; • Reform 5: Uniform in-service heavy vehicle standards; and • Reform 14: Adoption of national bus driving hours.	– Supplementary assessment of progress before 31 March 2000.
New South Wales	
– The dairy industry review panel was not sufficiently independent and the review did not clearly demonstrate that retaining market arrangements delivered a public benefit to the community as a whole (see section B5.4.2).	– Supplementary assessment before July 2000 taking into account the proposed national reform and adjustment package for the dairy industry.
– In principle agreement by New South Wales to reform domestic rice marketing arrangements consistent with review recommendation (continuing first tranche issue) and Working Group recommendation (see section B5.4.2).	– Supplementary assessment before July 2000.
– Legislation to provide for comprehensive system of water entitlements and trading not in place (see section B10.2.4).	– Supplementary assessment before July 2000 to review whether the legislation is in place.
Victoria	
– Retention of 8 per cent cap on the number of packaged liquor licences able to be held by an individual or company contrary to a review recommendation (see section B5.4.4).	– If the 8 per cent rule is not removed by 31 December 2000, the Council will consider an annual deduction from NCP payments.
– Retention of monopoly delivery of its compulsory third party (CTP) motor vehicle insurance contrary to review recommendations (see section B5.4.5).	– Victoria has undertaken to support a national review of motor vehicle CTP arrangements by the Productivity Commission. The Council will conduct a supplementary assessment if national review not progressed by July 2000.

Table A.4. Second tranche issues subject to supplementary assessment (cont.)

Second tranche issues	Comment
– Retention of monopoly delivery of workers' compensation arrangements contrary to review recommendations (see section B5.4.6).	– Victoria has agreed to support a national review of workers' compensation arrangements by the Productivity Commission. The Council will conduct a supplementary assessment if national review not progressed by July 2000.
– Retention of statutory monopoly in the provision of professional indemnity insurance for solicitors reverses an earlier decision to introduce competition as recommended by a review (see section B5.4.7).	– The Government has undertaken to conduct a further review to determine if changes are appropriate. The Council will conduct a supplementary assessment before July 2000.
– Questions about the implementation of competitive neutrality principles arising from the Coachtrans competitive neutrality complaint concerning Queensland rail (see section B3.3).	– A supplementary assessment will consider the implications of the Coachtrans complaint and progress in developing a CSO framework for public transport in SE Qld as agreed by Queensland.
	– The Council will consider recommending a deduction from the second tranche competition payments if there is evidence that competitive neutrality principles are not being appropriately applied.
– The dairy industry review did not clearly demonstrate that retaining market arrangements delivered a public benefit to the community as a whole (see section B5.4.).	– Supplementary assessment of progress before July 2000 taking into account the proposed national reform and adjustment package for the dairy industry.
– Queensland's application of the National Gas Access Code is not operational (see section B3.2).	– Supplementary assessment of progress before July 2000.
– Incomplete implementation of road transport reforms (see section B9.4): • Reform 3: Uniform national driver licensing transactions; • Reform 5 Uniform in-service heavy vehicle standards; and • Reform 15: Simplified fee-free interstate conversion of driver l cences.	– The government has a clear programme for implementing the outstanding reforms. Supplementary assessment of progress before 31 March 2000.

Queensland

Table A4. **Second tranche issues subject to supplementary assessment** *(cont.)*

Second tranche issues	Comment
– Incomplete implementation of water reform (see section B10.4): • Cost and pricing reforms of urban (metropolitan and town) water and wastewater providers; • Implementation of the recommendations of independent reviews on the introduction of two part tariffs (consumption based pricing) by local government; • Devolution of irrigation management; and • Separation of water service providers from regulation, standard setting and resource management functions.	– Supplementary assessment of progress before 31 December 1999.
– Legislation to provide for comprehensive system of water entitlements and trading not in place (see section B10.4.4).	– Supplementary assessment before July 2000 to review whether legislation is in place.
Western Australia – The dairy industry review did not clearly demonstrate that retaining market arrangements delivered a public benefit to the community as a whole (see section B5.4.1).	– Supplementary assessment before July 2000 taking into account the proposed national reform and adjustment package for the dairy industry.
– Incomplete implementation of road transport reforms (see section B9.4): • Reform 2: Uniform or consistent national registration requirements for heavy vehicles; • Reform 3: Uniform national driver licensing transactions; • Reform 4: Vehicle operations; • Reform 5: Uniform in-service heavy vehicle standards; • Reform 9: Common and simplified driver licence categories; • Reform 13: Enhanced safe carriage and restraint of loads; and • Reform 15: Simplified fee-free interstate conversion of driver licences.	– The Government has a clear programme for implementing the outstanding reforms. Supplementary assessment of progress before 31 March 2000.
– Legislation to provide for comprehensive system of water entitlements and trading not in place (see section B10.5.4).	– Supplementary assessment before July 2000 to review whether legislation is in place.

Table A4. **Second tranche issues subject to supplementary assessment** *(cont.)*

	Second tranche issues	Comment
South Australia	– No clear interest case to support the retention of restrictions on retail shop trading arrangements (see section B5.4.3).	– Recommendations of the review are not provided and the Government's case as outlined in the Annual Report does not demonstrate a supporting community benefit case. If restrictions on trading arrangements are not removed or shown to be in the public interest by 31 December 2000, the Council will consider an annual deduction from NCP payments.
	– Review recommendations to retain restrictions on liquor licensing but to review the matter again within 3-4 years (see section B5.4.4)	– The Government has agreed to consider review of the 'needs based' criteria for licensing in 2000-01.
	– Progress with implementation of electricity reforms – establishing regulatory arrangements as recommended by a review of structural arrangements (see section B7.2.1).	– Supplementary assessment of progress before 31 December 1999.
	– Insufficient information or Government response to the recommendations of the *Cooper Basin (Ratification) Act 1975* review to ensure free and fair trade in gas (see section B8.2).	– The Government is due to respond prior to 30 June 1999, otherwise supplementary assessment before 31 December 1999.
	– Incomplete implementation of road transport reforms (see section B9.4): • Reform 2: Uniform or consistent national registration requirements for heavy vehicles; • Reform 3: Uniform national driver licensing transactions; • Reform 4: Vehicle operations; • Reform 8: National mass and dimension limits for heavy vehicles; and • Reform 15: Enhanced safe carriage and restraint of loads.	– The Government has a clear programme for implementing the outstanding reforms. Supplementary assessment of progress before 31 March 2000.
	– Progress with reforming commercial water pricing.	– Supplementary assessment of progress before 31 December 1999.
	– Further progress on commercial bulk and wastewater pricing (see section B10.6.2).	– Supplementary assessment of progress before 31 July 2000.

Table A4. **Second tranche issues subject to supplementary assessment** *(cont.)*

Second tranche issues	Comment
Tasmania	
– Progress for review of compulsory third party (CTP) motor vehicle insurance arrangements casts doubt over review recommendations to retain monopoly arrangement (see section B5.4.5).	– The Government has undertaken to support a national review of motor vehicle CTP arrangements by the Productivity Commission. The Council will conduct a supplementary assessment if national review not progressed by July 2000.

– Incomplete implementation of road transport reforms (see section B9.5):
  • Reform 2: Uniform or consistent national registration requirements for heavy vehicles;
  • Reform 3: Uniform national driver licensing transactions; and
  • Reform 6: Nationally consistent arrangements for managing truck driver fatigue; use of logbooks not mandated and no exemption approved.
	– Supplementary assessment of progress before 31 March 2000.

– Progress with water pricing reform and the devolution of irrigation management (see section B10.7).	– Supplementary assessment before 31 December 1999 to ensure provision of a two part tariff implementation timetable and review progress on participant involvement in management of irrigation schemes.

– Progress with the agreed water reform framework (see section B10.7):
  • Passage of legislation for comprehensive system of water entitlements, trading and institutional separation; and
  • Progress with pricing reform and CSOs provided by local government.
	– Supplementary assessment before July 2000 to review whether legislation is in place and progress achieved against pricing reform timetable.

Australian Capital Territory	
– The dairy industry review process did not clearly demonstrate that retaining market arrangements delivered a public benefit to the community as a whole (see section B5.4.1).	– Supplementary assessment before July 2000 taking into account the proposed national reform and adjustment package for the dairy industry.

Table A4. **Second tranche issues subject to supplementary assessment** *(cont.)*

Second tranche issues	Comment

– Incomplete implementation of transport reform (see section B9.5):
  • Reform 2: Uniform or consistent national registration requirements for heavy vehicles;
  • Reform 3: Uniform national driver licensing transactions;
  • Reform 4: Vehicle operators;
  • Reform 9: Common and simplified driver licence categories.
	– The Government has a clear programme for implementing the outstanding reforms. Supplementary assessment of progress before 31 March 2000.

Northern Territory – Incomplete implementation of transport reform (see section B9.5):
  • Reform 3: Uniform national driver licensing transactions: demerit points not implemented;
 	
– Progress with elements of the agreed water reform framework (see section B10.9):
  • Cost recovery and rates of return achieved by urban water and wastewater services and cross-subsidies;
  • Separation of all regulatory and service provision function;
  • Removal of ties between water property rights and particular price of land and thus removal of all barriers to trade;
  • Provision of an implementation programme for environmental allocations; and
  • Bulk water pricing and economic viability assessment processes
	– Northern Territory to determine approach to demerit points. Supplementary assessment of progress before 31 March 2000.
	
	– Supplementary assessment of progress by 3 December 1999.

Source: National Competition Council (1999c).

Table A5. **Progress of reviews scheduled by jurisdiction, at 31 March 1999**

	Reviews scheduled to date[1]	Reviews completed and reform implemented	Reviews completed but reform still to be implemented	Reviews underway	Reviews scheduled but not commenced	Total reviews scheduled over life of NCP
Commonwealth	67	27	13	17	10	105
New South Wales	143	44	16	65	18	178
Victoria	121	57	19	20	25	219
Queensland	68	26	5	24	13	137
Western Australia	164	43	49[2]	47	25	307
South Australia	121	28	13	73	7	181
Tasmania	186	95	18	47	26	238
ACT	161	36	20	43	62	241
Northern Territory	85	17	9	55	4	87
Total (all jurisdiction)	1 116	373	162	391	190	1 693

1. Data on reviews scheduled do not include Acts where jurisdictions' preliminary reviews indicated there were no significant restrictions.
2. The Western Australian Government has endorsed a response to 45 reviews but is yet to take legislative action to implement the approach endorsed.
Source: Jurisdictions' Annual Reports for 1999.

Annex IV

Calendar of main economic events

1998

October

Mutual Obligation was extended to school leavers who had been unemployed for three months. Initially Mutual Obligation was applied only to 18 to 24 year old job seekers who had been on unemployment payments for six months or more.

November

At the 13 November Special Premiers' Conference, Commonwealth, State and Territory Governments developed an *Agreement on Principles for the Reform of Commonwealth-State Financial Relations*. This Agreement established a set of guiding principles for progressing the reform of Commonwealth-State financial relations announced in *A New Tax System*. These reforms will provide the States and Territories (the States) with a stable and growing source of revenue in the form of the GST to fund important community services, while allowing the States to reduce their reliance on a range of narrow and growth reducing taxes.

December

The National Electricity Market commenced full operations on 13 December. The National Electricity Market is a competitive market for the wholesale supply and purchase of electricity in the Australian Capital Territory, New South Wales, Queensland, South Australia and Victoria, and is accompanied by a regime of open access to electricity transmission and distribution networks.

The Government announced a number of changes to the Job Network in response to matters raised in consultations with Job Network providers across Australia. The key initiatives were to: improve the income and cash flow of Job Network providers, extend current contracts by three months and provide assistance to a small number of less successful Job Network providers to withdraw from the market.

The Corporate Law Economic Reform Program Bill 1998 was reintroduced into the House of Representatives on 3 December 1998. The Bill implements the CLERP proposals on directors' duties and corporate governance, accounting standards, fundraising and takeovers. The Bill was referred to the Parliamentary Joint Committee on Corporations and Securities which reported on 12 May 1999. The Bill was debated and passed by the House of Representatives on 3 June 1999. During the debate the Government foreshadowed amending the Bill in the Senate in response to the Committee's recommendations. The Bill was passed by the Parliament on 20 October 1999.

1999

February

The Australian Communications Authority completed an auction of radio-frequency spectrum in the 28/31 GHz bands. The auction has provided an existing competitor in the telecommunications industry, AAPT, with spectrum to provide a broadband point to multipoint radiocommunications service capable of carrying telephony and advanced communications services such as data, pay TV, internet access and video teleconferencing. Total proceeds from the auction were in the order of A$ 66 million.

March

The Government sold the National Transmission Network, which transmits the radio and TV programmes of the ABC and SBS, to a US-owned company for A$ 650 million.

A consultation paper, entitled *Financial Products, Service Providers and Markets – An Integrated Framework*, was released on 3 March 1999. It builds on earlier proposals and considers implementation issues. The consultation paper contains proposals for a harmonised regime for the licensing of financial service providers, markets, clearing and settlement facilities and a harmonised disclosure regime for all financial products – including securities, derivatives, superannuation, life and general insurance and bank deposit products. The public consultation period closed on 16 April with 115 submissions being received in response to the consultation paper. The submissions, which were received from industry bodies, exchanges and individuals, addressed an enormous range of issues. It is anticipated that the draft legislation will be released before the end of 1999 for a three month public exposure period before its introduction.

April

At the 8 April 1999 Premiers' Conference Heads of Government signed an Intergovernmental Agreement on the Reform of Commonwealth-State Financial Relations. Under the Intergovernmental Agreement the States will receive all GST revenues while Financial Assistance Grants and safety net surcharge arrangements for alcohol, petroleum and tobacco will cease from 1 July 2000. The States will also fund and administer a First Home Owners Scheme and abolish accommodation taxes, Financial Institutions Duty, debits tax and a number of business stamp duties. For 1999-2000, and prior to the introduction of these reforms, the Commonwealth undertook to maintain the existing Financial Assistance Grants to the States in real per capita terms, subject to the States meeting their obligations under the Agreement to Implement the National Competition Policy and Related Reforms.

The Australian Industrial Relations Commission (AIRC) awarded a safety net increase of A$ 12 per week for award rates of pay up to and including A$ 510 per week and A$ 10 to those earning above A$ 510 per week. The increases are absorbable into all above-award payments and are estimated to directly effect around a quarter of the workforce. The increases become available once 12 months has elapsed since increases flowing from the AIRC's 1998 decision were provided.

A review of the first year of Job Network was released that reported the system to be outperforming the former Commonwealth Employment Service by almost 50 per cent. In its first year, Job Network had over 500 000 vacancies lodged on the national vacancy database, and had placed 240 000 eligible job seekers under Job Matching including 12 500 Job Search Training and 70 000 Intensive Assistance placements.

May

The Victorian Government completed the privatisation of its gas industry assets, receiving approximately A$ 6.3 billion from the sale process. The privatised gas companies consisted of three stapled gas distribution and retail companies, and a gas transmission pipeline business.

The 1999-2000 Budget was delivered by the Treasurer. The 1999-2000 Budget is the first Commonwealth budget to be prepared using an accrual framework. In accrual terms, a fiscal surplus of A$ 5.4 billion, or 0.9 per cent of GDP, was forecast for 1999-2000. In cash terms, an underlying surplus of A$ 5.2 billion was forecast for 1999-2000. This is consistent with the Government's medium-term fiscal strategy of maintaining fiscal balance, on average, over the course of the economic cycle.

The Government announced some variations to its tax reform package of 13 August 1998, *not a new tax*, A *New Tax System*. Key elements remain unchanged. The Goods and Services Tax would remain at 10 per cent but basic food would be GST-free. Significant personal income tax cuts would remain for low and middle income earners with some paring back for higher income earners. The families package would be extended further and compensation through the social security system for low-income earners will be enhanced.

The Prime Minister and the Minister for Financial Services and Regulation, Mr. Hockey announced the Government's strategy to promote Australia as a centre for global financial services (CGFS). The Government's key role in promoting Australia as a CGFS is to ensure that the overall economic and regulatory framework continues to be of international best practice. The implementation of the A *New Tax System* reform proposals, the progression of business tax reform in the context of the Ralph Review of Business Taxation, and the maintenance of sound macroeconomic policy settings are crucial elements in that framework. The Government will also play an important role in facilitating more effective and coordinated promotion of Australia as a CGFS. To do this, the 1999-2000 Budget provided A$ 7 million over two years to fund this promotional strategy.

June

Legislation to implement the second stage of the Government's response to the Financial System Inquiry was passed in June 1999.

The first stage of the reforms introduced a new organisational framework for the regulation of the financial system from 1 July 1998 and a variety of measures to improve efficiency and contestability in financial markets and the payments system.

This second stage of reforms:

- involved the transfer of regulatory responsibility for building societies, credit unions and friendly societies from the States and Territories to the Commonwealth;
- brought the regulation of building societies and credit unions into line with the regulation of other authorised deposit-taking institutions (including banks);
- established a mechanism to facilitate the quick and efficient transfer of business from one authorised deposit-taking institution to another, providing an effective prudential regulation tool in cases of financial distress, with the aim of preventing losses and maintaining confidence in the financial sector; and
- established a single regulatory framework for life insurance companies and friendly societies while recognising the special features of friendly societies.

In particular, these reforms will enable the non-bank deposit-taking sector to provide a more effective source of competition for the banks in the retail market by operating under the same regulatory structure as banks. These institutions will be able to maintain commercial flexibility by retaining different corporate structures, including mutuality, and the terms "building society", "credit union" and "friendly society".

Changes to the GST base announced by the Prime Minister on 28 May 1999 necessitated some adjustments to the Intergovernmental Agreement that was signed at the April 1999 Premiers' Conference. In June 1999, Heads of Government agreed upon a revised Intergovernmental Agreement that incorporated these amendments.

The second Job Network Request for Tender to provide about A$ 3 billion worth of employment services for the three year period commencing 28 February 2000 was released, with successful tenders to be announced by December 1999. Changes to the tender included: introducing managed price competition for Intensive Assistance; increased accountability requirements from Job Network providers for Intensive Assistance; a new bonus for Job Search Training placements; and an increased focus on quality of services.

The *Workplace Relations Legislation Amendment (More Jobs, Better Pay) Bill* 1999 was introduced into Parliament. The Bill builds upon the Government's existing workplace relations reforms by introducing a range of measures to further improve the flexibility and efficiency of the labour market. Key elements of reform include increasing the incentive to bargain; reducing the role of third parties; strengthening further the existing freedom of association provisions; expanding the AIRC's powers to stop or prevent industrial action; and introducing secret ballots prior to protected action.

Legislation giving effect to the Government's new tax system was passed by the Australian Parliament.

July

Based on advice from the National Competition Council (NCC), the Treasurer announced that competition payments amounting to approximately A$ 624 million would be made to the States and Territories, for the period 1999-2000, in recognition of the progress they had made in implementing National Competition Policy and Related Reforms. In relation to Queensland, A$ 14.83 million in payments have been suspended pending further assessment by the Council (before 31 December 1999) regarding compliance with a specific water reform requirement. It was announced that State and Territory payments for 2000-01 (a maximum A$ 450 million) will be determined following a series of supplementary assessments covering a range of reform commitments to be completed by June 2000.

The Australian Competition and Consumer Commission's new price monitoring powers under Part VB of the *Trade Practices Act* 1974 commenced. The Commission's powers aim to prevent price exploitation during the transition to the goods and services tax.

Mutual Obligation was extended to long-term unemployed people aged between 25 and 34 years of age. As a result, the number of Work for the Dole places will double from 25 000 in 1998-99 to 50 000 by 2000-01. The range of options for eligible unemployed to meet their mutual obligation was also widened.

The Review of Business Taxation, established by the Government in August 1998 to provide a consultative forum for consideration of new business taxation arrangements outlined in *A New Tax System*, completed its report to the Government. The 800 page report, along with two public discussion papers and an information paper released in the course of the Review, provides a comprehensive analysis of existing business tax arrangements as well as over 280 recommendations for reform based on the Government's earlier proposals.

August

On 4 August 1999, following a Joint Prime Ministerial Task Force on Australia New Zealand Bilateral Relations, the Prime Minister announced changes to Australia's foreign investment policy. The changes increase the notification threshold for foreign investment in existing businesses from A$ 5 million (A$ 3 million for rural businesses) to A$ 50 million; remove foreign investment approval requirements for individuals, who hold or are entitled to hold a special category visa and invest in Australian residential real estate through Australian companies and trusts; and increase the limit for which applications for investment in businesses are registered, but are generally not fully examined, from A$ 50 million to A$ 100 million.

September

Consistent with the foreign investment policy measures announced on 4 August 1999 by the Prime Minister, on 3 September 1999 the Treasurer announced that the Government had also decided to increase the voluntary notification threshold to A$ 50 million (from A$ 20 million) for the Australian assets of an offshore company to be acquired by another offshore company. The Government also decided to exempt acquisitions of residential real estate by Australian permanent resident visa holders, not ordinarily resident in Australia, purchasing through Australian companies or trusts. Modifications to foreign investment policy were also made to the treatment of vacant land and housing packages; the treatment of developed non-residential commercial property; the designation of integrated tourism resorts; the sale of strata titled hotel accommodation; Australian citizens and their foreign spouses purchasing as joint tenants, and foreign trustees' acquisition of interests in urban land. Where properties are not subject to heritage listing, the notification threshold applying to the acquisition of developed non-residential commercial properties will be raised from A$ 5 million to A$ 50 million. Acquisitions of such properties valued up to A$ 100 million will no longer be subject to detailed examination, unless the facts of the proposal raise issues pertaining to the national interest.

The Government announced the development of a Green Paper on welfare reform, with a final draft to be provided to the Minister for Family and Community Services by June 2000. The Green Paper will develop options to prevent and reduce welfare dependency.

The Government announced its initial response to the report of the Review of Business Taxation. Key changes announced included: a reduction in the company tax rate to 34 per cent in 2000-01 and 30 per cent from 2001-02; removal of accelerated depreciation arrangements in favour of effective life arrangements; more internationally competitive capital gains tax arrangements, including exemption for non-resident tax exempt pension funds in respect of venture capital investments; a Simplified Tax System for small business; a range of integrity measures designed to improve the fairness of the system; and new entity tax arrangements broadly in line with those outlined in A New Tax System. These arrangements are designed to provide Australia with a modern, competitive and fair business tax system. The Government has foreshadowed that it will be considering remaining recommendations in the Review's report with a view to a further announcement in November.

The Final Budget Outcome for FY 1998-99 was an underlying cash surplus of A$ 4.2 billion (0.7 per cent of GDP). This compares with an underlying surplus of A$ 2.9 billion estimated at the time of the 1999-2000 Budget. This outcome was predominantly due to lower than anticipated outlays.

The Choice of Superannuation Funds (Consumer Protection) Bill was introduced into the House of Representatives on 23 September 1999 and debated and passed on 21 October 1999. The Bill will strengthen consumer protection in the life insurance industry; enhance the accountability of life companies and life brokers in respect of product distribution; and improve consistency in the regulatory treatment of life insurance advisers, securities dealers and their representatives. The Bill is now being considered by the Senate.

October

The Corporate Law Economic Reform Program Bill 1998 was passed by the Commonwealth Parliament. The Bill is a key part of the Government's programme to modernise the regulation of business and financial markets, and covers the areas of Directors' Duties and Corporate Governance, Fundraising, Accounting Standards and Takeovers.

The Government sold a further 16.6 per cent of the Commonwealth's equity in Telstra Corporation in a public float which will raise over A$ 16 billion in sale proceeds. A$ 1 billion of the sale proceeds will be used to improve telecommunications and the environment in regional Australia. The remainder of the proceeds of the sale will be used to repay Commonwealth Government debt. The Commonwealth still retains majority ownership of Telstra with a 50.1 per cent stake in the corporation.

The Workplace Relations Legislation Amendment (Youth Employment) Act 1999 came into operation. It permanently exempts junior rates of pay from anti-discrimination provisions of the Workplace Relations Act 1996 (the Act). The legislation also extends the exemption to traineeships and apprenticeships, which were previously excluded from the exemption.

STATISTICAL ANNEX AND STRUCTURAL INDICATORS

Table A. **Selected background statistics**

	Average 1989-98	1989	1990	1991	1992	1993	1994	1995	1996	1997	1998
A.	**Percentage changes from previous year at constant 1997-98 prices**										
Private consumption	3.4	5.8	2.9	0.7	2.7	1.8	4.0	5.1	3.3	3.9	4.3
Gross fixed capital formation	4.1	10.8	-7.8	-9.0	2.8	4.8	12.7	4.0	5.7	11.4	6.1
Public sector	1.0	17.8	4.9	-5.7	-3.7	-2.8	6.5	0.2	-0.1	0.9	-8.3
of which: Public enterprises	-2.7	20.5	7.9	-11.8	-6.6	-9.2	5.1	2.8	-7.5	-6.6	-21.3
Private sector	4.9	9.0	-11.3	-10.1	5.1	7.3	14.7	4.5	6.8	14.3	9.1
of which:											
Residential	4.3	8.7	-11.3	-6.2	13.1	13.3	11.9	-5.9	-7.5	14.4	12.6
Non-residential construction	4.7	11.4	-8.8	-19.7	-13.0	-2.8	7.9	18.9	18.0	8.8	26.4
Machine and equipment and intangible assets	6.8	13.1	-12.4	-9.7	8.0	7.0	20.3	10.1	11.9	17.1	2.1
GDP	3.4	4.4	1.5	-1.0	2.6	3.8	5.0	4.4	4.0	3.9	5.1
GDP deflator	2.3	6.9	4.9	2.6	1.4	1.4	0.9	1.5	2.0	1.4	0.3
Employment	1.5	4.3	1.8	-2.3	-0.5	0.6	3.1	4.0	1.3	1.0	2.1
Compensation of employees (current prices)	6.1	13.1	9.0	1.0	3.0	3.3	7.0	7.2	6.7	5.0	5.7
Productivity (real GDP/employment)	1.8	0.1	-0.3	1.4	3.1	3.3	1.8	0.4	2.7	2.8	2.9
Unit labour costs (compensation/real GDP)	2.7	8.3	7.5	2.0	0.4	-0.5	1.9	2.7	2.6	1.1	0.6
B.	**Percentage ratios**										
Gross fixed capital formation as % of GDP (constant prices)	21.6	23.7	21.5	19.8	19.8	20.0	21.5	21.4	21.8	23.3	23.6
Stockbuilding as % of GDP (constant prices)	0.3	1.6	0.3	-1.0	-0.4	0.6	0.3	0.8	0.6	-1.0	0.7
Foreign balance as % of GDP (constant prices)	-0.5	-3.6	-1.8	0.5	0.2	0.8	0.1	-0.5	0.0	0.2	-1.1
Compensation of employees as % of GDP (current prices)	47.9	47.4	48.6	48.3	47.8	46.9	47.4	48.0	48.2	48.1	48.2
Direct taxes as per cent of household income	19.9	22.1	20.5	19.6	18.3	18.7	18.4	19.4	19.9	20.8	21.8
Unemployment as per cent of total labour force	8.8	6.2	6.9	9.6	10.8	10.9	9.7	8.5	8.5	8.6	8.0
C.	**Other indicator**										
Current balance (US$ billion)	-14.9	-18.3	-16.0	-11.2	-11.2	-9.8	-17.2	-19.6	-15.8	-12.7	-17.6

Source: Australian Bureau of Statistics and OECD Secretariat.

Table B. Gross domestic product

A-$ million

	1989	1990	1991	1992	1993	1994	1995	1996	1997	1998
					Current prices					
Private consumption	206 988	226 596	237 868	249 857	260 428	273 316	292 501	307 528	323 937	342 307
Government consumption expenditure	66 897	73 701	78 997	82 440	85 166	88 453	92 844	96 885	100 256	104 784
Gross fixed capital formation	88 650	93 843	85 543	83 225	94 188	106 442	111 185	116 541	127 520	137 804
Private sector	76 934	70 094	62 465	65 933	72 546	83 662	88 036	93 558	104 654	116 537
Public enterprises	12 198	3 737	2 472	1 690	10 524	11 117	11 654	10 912	10 158	8 152
General government	9 518	10 012	10 612	10 601	11 018	11 663	11 496	12 072	12 709	13 115
Increase in stocks	5 528	461	-3 012	-1 464	2 023	2 393	2 490	1 659	-4 049	3 276
Exports of goods and services	53 204	63 810	68 491	77 604	80 294	84 089	93 561	100 826	112 347	114 562
Imports of goods and services	67 948	67 904	67 123	74 916	82 531	90 197	100 567	101 690	110 485	125 092
Statistical discrepancy	592	3 354	-879	-1 637	-1 453	-359	-426	-47	-244	1 469
Gross domestic product	369 908	393 562	399 891	415 110	438 114	464 138	491 587	521 702	549 282	579 111
Indirect taxes less subsidies	41 400	43 579	43 120	45 315	46 276	53 439	56 532	59 836	63 956	66 079
Statistical discrepancy (GDP by cost)	-67	540	3 457	5 150	3 529	869	-129	-252	1 054	-3 194
Gross domestic product at factor cost	328 576	349 544	353 314	364 645	388 310	409 829	435 185	462 118	484 271	516 224
					Average 1997-98 prices					
Private consumption	256 732	264 226	266 049	273 197	278 114	289 172	303 784	313 940	326 064	340 025
Government consumption expenditure	83 754	86 686	88 821	89 666	90 073	93 568	96 917	99 102	100 999	103 693
Gross fixed capital formation	103 208	95 113	86 555	88 950	93 241	105 066	109 312	115 506	128 684	136 510
Private sector	80 310	71 218	64 032	67 288	72 220	82 818	86 535	92 443	105 690	115 317
Public enterprises	13 513	14 632	12 947	12 097	12 980	11 542	11 869	10 981	10 252	8 069
General government	9 754	9 857	10 121	10 591	10 554	11 355	11 089	11 908	12 823	13 100
Increase in stocks	7 050	1 538	-4 271	-1 534	2 743	1 638	3 863	2 925	-5 577	3 833
Exports of goods and services	58 364	63 317	71 604	75 452	81 510	83 864	93 362	103 287	115 213	114 792
Imports of goods and services	74 207	71 225	69 479	74 424	77 569	88 532	95 667	103 485	114 191	120 978
Statistical discrepancy	1 911	3 785	-935	-1 758	-1 539	-187	-664	-40	92	1 237
Gross domestic product	435 177	441 560	437 238	448 475	465 685	489 118	510 405	530 829	551 271	579 255

Source: Australian Bureau of Statistics.

Table C. **Income and expenditure of households[1]**

A$ million, current prices

	1989	1990	1991	1992	1993	1994	1995	1996	1997	1998
Compensation of employees	175 287	191 169	193 077	199 038	205 655	220 055	235 874	251 582	264 206	279 180
Income from property and entrepreneurship	123 190	128 866	121 685	116 814	116 990	123 154	135 343	141 869	142 543	149 730
Gross operating surplus – dwellings owned by persons	28 617	31 699	33 457	34 313	35 422	36 414	39 056	42 131	45 593	47 609
Gross mixed income	43 933	41 650	39 950	42 013	44 617	46 110	49 541	51 655	52 659	56 483
Property income received[2]	50 640	55 517	48 278	40 488	36 951	40 630	46 746	48 083	44 291	45 638
Social benefits receivable	26 978	30 692	35 269	39 413	41 816	43 836	46 596	50 278	51 264	51 970
Workers' compensation	3 521	3 592	3 789	4 050	4 033	4 313	4 700	4 908	5 023	5 153
Social assistance benefits	23 457	27 100	31 480	35 363	37 783	39 523	41 896	45 370	46 241	46 817
Non-life insurance claims	8 128	9 175	9 495	8 947	9 127	10 587	11 710	12 581	13 345	13 938
Current transfers to non-profit institutions	4 104	4 708	5 091	5 647	6 050	6 789	8 061	8 266	9 397	9 716
Other current transfers	749	774	793	804	813	850	916	977	1 002	952
Non-residents	747	772	793	804	811	848	914	906	916	936
Other sectors	2	2	0	0	2	2	2	71	86	16
Income receivable	338 436	365 384	365 410	370 663	380 451	405 271	438 500	465 553	481 757	505 486
Property income payable	28 781	31 902	27 385	21 146	19 572	20 810	26 570	27 889	26 387	28 166
Dwellings and unincorporated enterprises	22 166	25 198	22 613	18 138	16 989	17 786	22 361	23 363	21 789	23 275
Consumer debt income	6 615	6 704	4 772	3 008	2 583	3 024	4 209	4 526	4 598	4 891
Income tax payable	48 773	49 754	48 421	47 071	49 228	51 681	58 141	63 200	68 239	74 149
Other current taxes on income, wealth, etc.	961	976	1 039	1 279	1 476	1 603	1 623	1 694	1 872	1 952
Social contributions for workers' compensation	3 519	3 841	3 743	3 778	3 742	4 060	4 578	4 829	4 986	5 127
Net non-life insurance premiums	7 592	7 608	8 107	8 753	9 407	9 792	10 361	11 315	12 101	12 855
Other current transfers	844	940	1 039	1 078	1 091	1 124	1 211	1 332	1 345	1 432
Non-residents	495	522	535	540	549	583	623	644	668	686
Other sectors	349	418	504	538	542	541	588	688	677	746
Income payable	90 470	95 021	89 734	83 105	84 516	89 070	102 484	110 259	114 930	123 681
Gross disposable income	247 966	270 365	275 676	287 559	295 934	316 201	336 016	355 293	366 827	381 803
Consumption expenditure	206 988	226 396	237 868	249 857	260 428	273 316	292 501	307 528	323 937	342 307
Net saving[3]	18 366	21 580	15 040	13 940	10 166	16 174	15 798	19 248	12 952	7 441
Consumption of fixed capital	22 612	22 389	22 768	23 762	25 340	26 711	27 717	28 517	29 938	32 055
Net saving as a percentage of net disposable income	8.1	8.7	5.9	5.3	3.8	5.6	5.1	5.9	3.8	2.1

1. Includes non-profit institutions serving households and unincorporated enterprises.
2. Includes investment income of insurance enterprises and superannuation funds attributable to policyholders and imputed interest on government unfunded superannuation arrangements.
3. Net saving is derived as a balancing item.
Source: Australian Bureau of Statistics.

Table D. **Prices and wages**

	1989	1990	1991	1992	1993	1994	1995	1996	1997	1998
					Index FY 1997-98 = 100					
Price deflators										
Gross domestic product	85.0	89.2	91.5	92.8	94.1	94.9	96.3	98.3	99.6	100.0
Private consumption	80.5	85.7	89.4	91.5	93.6	94.5	96.3	98.0	99.3	100.7
Gross fixed capital formation	95.6	98.7	98.8	99.2	101.0	101.3	101.7	100.9	99.1	100.9
Exports[1]	99.7	100.8	95.7	97.6	98.5	94.6	100.2	97.6	97.5	99.8
Imports[1]	91.6	95.1	96.6	100.7	106.4	101.9	105.1	98.3	96.8	103.4
Terms of trade[1]	108.9	105.7	99.0	96.9	92.6	92.9	95.3	99.3	100.8	96.5
Consumer price index[2]										
Total	80.0	85.8	88.6	89.4	91.1	92.8	97.1	99.6	99.9	100.7
Total less food	80.0	86.4	89.1	89.9	91.4	93.3	97.7	100.3	100.0	100.5
Food	79.8	83.3	86.1	87.3	89.4	90.5	94.0	96.6	99.1	101.8
Average weekly earnings, all employees	75.3	80.2	83.3	85.3	87.7	90.3	92.8	95.6	98.6	101.3

1. Goods and services.
2. Not adjusted for the effects of Medicare.
Source: Australian Bureau of Statistics and OECD, *Main Economic Indicators*.

Table E. **Balance of payments**

A$ million

	1990	1991	1992	1993	1994	1995	1996	1997	1998
Exports goods	50 748	54 376	58 354	62 728	64 695	71 785	77 122	87 435	88 902
Imports goods	-50 278	-49 837	-56 163	-62 795	-69 086	-77 484	-77 935	-85 054	-97 527
Trade balance	470	4 539	2 191	-67	-4 391	-5 699	-813	2 381	-8 625
Services, net	-21 430	-18 801	-17 213	-14 048	-18 557	-20 424	-19 507	-19 186	-19 257
Non-factor services, credit	13 062	14 115	15 250	17 566	19 394	21 776	23 704	24 912	25 660
Non-factor services, debit	-17 626	-17 286	-18 753	-19 736	-21 111	-23 083	-23 755	-25 431	-27 565
Non-factor-services, net	-4 564	-3 171	-3 503	-2 170	-1 717	-1 307	-51	-519	-1 905
Investment income, credit	4 137	4 216	5 159	6 144	6 084	7 103	7 691	9 670	10 554
Investment income, debit	-21 003	-19 846	-18 869	-18 022	-22 924	-26 220	-27 147	-28 337	-27 906
Investment income, net	-16 866	-15 630	-13 710	-11 878	-16 840	-19 117	-19 456	-18 667	-17 352
Balance on goods and services	-20 960	-14 262	-15 022	-14 115	-22 948	-26 123	-20 320	-16 805	-27 882
Transfers credits	2 958	2 753	2 915	3 089	3 017	3 189	3 427	3 695	4 032
Transfers debits	-2 506	-2 847	-3 154	-3 429	-3 536	-3 537	-3 280	-3 951	-4 133
Unrequited transfers, net	452	-94	-239	-340	-519	-348	147	-256	-101
Balance on current account	-20 508	-14 356	-15 261	-14 455	-23 467	-26 471	-20 173	-17 061	-27 983
Net capital movements[1]	19 237	14 014	16 847	13 298	21 453	27 183	20 146	16 504	28 083
Net errors and omissions	1 271	342	-1 586	1 157	2 014	-712	27	557	-100
Changes in official reserves	-2 236	427	6 393	28	1 218	-491	-3 076	-4 746	2 886

1. Including changes in official reserves.
Source: Australian Bureau of Statistics and OECD, Main Economics Indicators.

Table F. Foreign trade by commodity[1]

SITC sections:	US$ millions							Per cent of total						
	1980	1985	1990	1995	1996	1997	1998	1980	1985	1990	1995	1996	1997	1998
Total exports, fob	22 190	22 604	39 753	53 121	60 539	62 833	55 885	100.0	100.0	100.0	100.0	100.0	100.0	100.0
0. Food and live animals	7 545	5 350	7 587	9 692	12 368	12 772	9 507	34.0	23.7	19.1	18.2	20.4	20.3	17.0
1. Beverages and tobacco	48	50	223	431	578	657	724	0.2	0.2	0.6	0.8	1.0	1.0	1.3
2. Crude materials, inedible, except fuels	6 464	6 225	10 509	10 844	11 759	12 680	11 258	29.1	27.5	26.4	20.4	19.4	20.2	20.1
3. Mineral fuels, lubricants and related materials	2 408	5 891	7 501	8 880	10 184	11 090	9 483	10.8	26.1	18.9	16.7	16.8	17.6	17.0
4. Animal and vegetable oils, fats and waxes	115	95	102	190	187	199	243	0.5	0.4	0.3	0.4	0.3	0.3	0.4
5. Chemicals and related products, n.e.s.	480	402	1 013	2 154	2 351	2 383	2 121	2.2	1.8	2.5	4.1	3.9	3.8	3.8
6. Manufactured goods classified chiefly by material	2 575	2 268	4 891	7 257	7 392	7 378	6 565	11.6	10.0	12.3	13.7	12.2	11.7	11.7
7. Machinery and transport equipment	1 176	1 072	3 220	6 787	7 812	8 362	6 712	5.3	4.7	8.1	12.8	12.9	13.3	12.0
8. Miscellaneous manufactured articles	384	432	1 020	1 849	2 205	2 276	2 073	1.7	1.9	2.6	3.5	3.6	3.6	3.7
9. Commodities and transactions not elsewhere classified	1 012	817	3 685	5 037	5 703	5 036	7 198	4.6	3.6	9.3	9.5	9.4	8.0	12.9
Total imports, cif	20 251	23 153	38 913	57 425	61 406	61 845	60 821	100.0	100.0	100.0	100.0	100.0	100.0	100.0
0. Food and live animals	904	1 503	1 495	2 184	2 285	2 365	2 302	4.5	6.5	3.8	3.8	3.7	3.8	3.8
1. Beverages and tobacco	185	189	315	374	402	400	369	0.9	0.8	0.8	0.7	0.7	0.6	0.6
2. Crude materials, inedible, except fuels	876	685	1 096	1 297	1 183	1 156	1 020	4.3	3.0	2.8	2.3	1.9	1.9	1.7
3. Mineral fuels, lubricants and related materials	2 791	1 577	2 191	2 880	3 839	3 750	2 702	13.8	6.8	5.6	5.0	6.3	6.1	4.4
4. Animal and vegetable oils, fats and waxes	80	75	98	186	208	202	170	0.4	0.3	0.3	0.3	0.3	0.3	0.3
5. Chemicals and related products, n.e.s.	1 755	1 773	4 005	6 369	7 102	6 384	6 941	8.7	7.7	10.3	11.1	11.6	11.3	11.4
6. Manufactured goods classified chiefly by material	3 543	3 690	5 964	8 442	8 306	8 351	8 185	17.5	15.9	15.3	14.7	13.5	13.8	13.5
7. Machinery and transport equipment	7 293	9 778	17 491	26 975	28 840	28 578	27 888	36.0	42.2	44.9	47.0	47.0	46.4	45.9
8. Miscellaneous manufactured articles	2 457	3 092	5 410	8 130	8 653	9 108	9 125	12.1	13.4	13.9	14.2	14.1	14.7	15.0
9. Commodities and transactions not elsewhere classified	356	792	854	515	589	650	2 119	1.8	3.4	2.2	1.1	1.0	1.1	3.5

1. General trade.
Source: OECD, Foreign Trade Statistics, Series A.

Table G. **Foreign trade by area**[1]

US$ million

	1988	1989	1990	1991	1992	1993	1994	1995	1996	1997	1998
Exports, fob											
OECD Europe	5 438	5 941	6 277	5 972	6 218	5 541	5 624	6 478	7 495	7 341	8 923
of which: United Kingdom	1 166	1 323	1 400	1 330	1 665	1 910	1 711	1 829	2 124	1 803	2 945
OECD North America	4 137	4 469	5 011	4 901	4 474	4 335	4 265	4 296	4 923	5 660	6 340
Japan	8 882	9 761	10 206	11 538	10 714	10 441	11 613	12 182	12 080	12 458	10 940
Korea	1 532	1 893	2 202	2 629	2 642	2 914	3 424	4 473	5 708	5 028	3 830
New Zealand	1 626	1 890	1 954	2 040	2 236	2 463	3 149	3 832	4 278	4 591	3 576
Far East	6 936	7 937	8 476	10 439	11 941	12 034	14 103	16 415	18 492	20 392	15 584
Other non-OECD countries	3 652	4 335	3 826	3 570	3 374	3 603	3 950	4 163	5 874	6 593	6 000
Non-specified	465	763	958	841	835	1 058	1 300	1 120	1 370	750	678
Total	32 671	36 991	38 912	41 934	42 439	42 392	47 432	52 968	60 225	62 822	55 885
Imports, cif											
OECD Europe	9 449	10 885	10 681	9 639	9 986	10 065	12 644	15 600	16 265	16 043	15 469
of which: United Kingdom	2 467	2 785	2 701	2 401	2 413	2 410	2 979	3 451	3 921	3 960	3 633
OECD North America	8 043	10 320	10 309	10 180	9 993	9 896	11 934	13 809	15 628	14 740	14 828
Japan	6 713	8 320	7 307	6 808	7 373	8 073	8 867	8 878	8 000	8 453	8 369
Korea	868	1 068	934	985	1 103	1 265	1 297	1 674	1 822	2 168	2 618
New Zealand	1 463	1 662	1 715	1 768	1 876	2 065	2 482	2 672	2 881	2 749	2 402
Far East	5 067	6 231	5 773	6 748	7 636	7 948	9 624	11 101	12 710	13 671	14 240
Other non-OECD countries	1 680	2 370	2 355	2 524	2 722	3 040	3 033	3 653	4 010	3 751	2 646
Non-specified	56	92	63	70	67	71	71	79	158	270	162
Total	33 340	40 949	39 139	38 723	40 756	42 422	49 952	57 465	61 475	61 846	60 821

1. General trade.
Source: OECD, *Foreign trade Statistics,* Series A.

Table H. **Production structure and performance indicators**

Fiscal years[1]

	1975	1980	1985	1990	1995	1998	1975	1980	1985	1990	1995	1998
	GDP share						Employment share					
A. Production structure (constant prices)												
Tradeables												
Agriculture, forestry and fishing	3.9	3.1	3.4	3.4	3.1	3.2	6.9	6.5	5.9	5.6	4.8	4.9
Mining and quarrying	3.2	3.0	3.6	4.2	4.6	4.3	1.3	1.3	1.4	1.3	1.1	1.0
Manufacturing	18.0	17.5	15.2	14.6	13.3	12.3	23.5	20.1	16.9	15.0	13.4	12.8
Non-tradeables												
Electricity, gas and water	2.3	2.5	2.7	2.8	2.5	2.3	1.8	2.1	2.0	1.4	1.0	0.8
Construction	6.7	6.6	6.6	5.7	5.3	5.8	8.6	7.8	7.4	7.3	7.3	7.2
Trade, restaurants and hotels	14.3	13.7	13.0	12.2	12.6	12.7	19.9	20.4	23.2	25.1	25.6	25.6
Transport, storage and communication	5.6	6.6	7.0	7.3	8.3	8.5	7.6	7.5	7.7	6.7	6.6	6.3
Finance, insurance, real estate and business services[2]	19.5	20.8	21.6	24.3	24.2	25.5	7.3	8.1	10.7	12.4	13.5	14.5
Community, social and personal services	9.4	9.5	9.8	10.3	9.7	9.5	18.8	21.8	13.1	13.8	15.2	15.9
Other[3]	9.3	9.6	9.5	9.3	9.1	8.4	4.3	4.4	11.6	11.6	11.5	10.9

	1975	1980	1985	1990	1995	1998	1975	1980	1985	1990	1995	1998
	Productivity growth[4]						Investment share					
B. Economic performance (constant prices)												
Tradeables												
Agriculture, forestry and fishing	..	2.8	2.7	−0.7	−2.5	10.0	4.7	4.8	4.7	4.7	4.5	4.5
Mining and quarrying	..	−0.9	1.8	5.2	8.1	7.4	9.4	9.4	9.4	9.3	9.1	11.7
Manufacturing	..	3.9	2.2	1.8	2.3	1.7	9.7	9.7	9.7	9.6	10.1	10.1
Non-tradeables												
Electricity, gas and water	..	0.8	3.0	9.1	7.0	12.6	5.2	5.2	5.2	5.2	5.1	2.5
Construction	..	3.4	2.0	−0.5	0.9	5.1	2.2	2.2	2.2	2.2	2.5	2.8
Trade, restaurants and hotels	..	−0.3	−1.4	−1.6	1.0	2.7	7.5	7.5	7.5	7.4	8.6	10.1
Transport, storage and communication	..	3.8	2.5	3.6	4.6	4.5	14.0	14.1	14.0	13.9	14.0	12.3
Finance, insurance, real estate and business services[2]	..	0.3	−2.5	−0.4	0.8	0.6	36.6	36.7	36.6	36.2	34.9	35.1
Community, social and personal services	..	0.7	4.9	8.8	0.1	0.4	5.5	5.5	5.5	5.5	5.6	5.6
Other[3]	..	2.5	16.4	0.7	2.2	−0.4	5.2	4.8	5.2	6.0	5.8	5.4

	1980	1988	1989	1990	1991	1992	1993	1994	1995	1996	1997	1998
C. Other indicators (current prices)												
Effective rate of protection, manufacturing	23	17	15	14	13	12	10	9	8	6	..	..
R&D in per cent of GDP	1.0	1.3		1.4		1.6	..	1.6	..	1.7		
Levels of net foreign debt[5]/GDP	6.2	31.8	33.3	34.0	35.8	39.2	41.2	37.3	39.3	38.0	39.8	40.1
Levels of foreign direct investment[5]/GDP	16.4	21.1	23.8	24.0	24.5	25.8	26.7	26.5	26.0	26.8	28.1	27.5

1. Beginning 1st July of the year indicated
2. Including ownership of dwellings.
3. Government administration, defence and education
4. Average rate of growth between periods.
5. At 30 June of the year indicated.
Source: Australian Bureau of Statistics; Reserve Bank of Australia; OECD, *National Accounts* and *Main Science and Technology Indicators.*

Table I. **Labour market indicators**

	A. Evolution									
	Peak		Trough		1985	1990	1995	1996	1997	1998
Standardised unemployment rate (s.a)	1993	10.9	1981	5.8	8.3	7.0	8.5	8.6	8.5	8.0
Unemployment rate (s.a)										
Total	1993	10.9	1981	5.8	8.3	7.0	8.5	8.6	8.5	8.0
Male	1993	11.5	1981	4.8	7.9	6.8	8.8	8.8	8.7	8.2
Female	1983	10.4	1989	6.8	8.8	7.2	8.0	8.2	8.3	7.7
Youth[1]	1992	19.4	1989	11.1	15.2	13.0	15.3	15.6	16.2	15.1
Share of long-term unemployment[2]	1993	36.7	1982	18.8	30.8	21.1	32.0	28.5	30.9	32.0
Non-farm vacancies (thousand)	1998	74.8	1983	20.3	54.0	48.3	57.3	60.8	64.5	74.8
Average hours worked in manufacturing, weekly	1970	39.5	1983	35.6	37.0	38.2	38.8	38.7	38.6	38.6
Overtime hours per week, non-farm	1989	1.5	1998	1.0	1.2	1.3	1.2	1.1	1.1	1.0

	B. Structural of institutionnal characteristics							
	1970	1980	1985	1990	1995	1996	1997	1998
Labour force (percentage change)[3]	2.6	1.6	1.8	3.0	1.3	1.3	1.0	1.5
Participation rate[4]								
Total	..	61.3	60.8	63.8	63.7	63.6	63.2	63.3
Male	..	78.3	75.8	75.6	73.9	73.6	73.1	72.9
Female	..	44.8	46.3	52.2	53.7	53.8	53.7	53.9
Employment by sector								
Per cent of total								
Agriculture	8.0	6.5	6.2	5.6	5.0	5.0	5.1	4.9
Industry	37.0	31.0	27.6	25.1	22.9	22.5	22.1	21.7
Services	55.0	62.5	66.4	69.0	71.9	72.3	72.3	72.9
Percentage change[3]								
Agriculture	−0.8	0.1	0.3	1.2	−1.4	2.5	2.7	−2.3
Industry	2.3	−0.3	−1.0	1.4	−0.9	−0.5	−0.6	0.3
Services	3.3	2.4	2.5	4.0	1.8	1.8	1.0	2.8
Total	2.6	1.4	1.3	3.2	0.9	1.3	1.0	2.1
Part-time employment, per cent of total employed	..	15.9	17.9	21.2	24.5	24.8	25.5	25.7

1. People between 15 and 24 years as a percentage of the labour force of the same age group.
2. People looking for a job since one year or more as a percentage of total unemployment.
3. Average rate of growth between periods.
4. Labour force as a percentage of the corresponding population aged 15 and over.
Source: Australian Bureau of Statistics and OECD, *Labour Force Statistics.*

Table J. **The public sector**

A$ million, current prices

	1980	1985	1990	1995	1996	1997	1998
General government accounts							
Direct taxes	21 195	37 824	69 391	80 626	87 029	93 873	103 257
Household direct taxes	15 824	30 066	49 754	58 141	63 200	68 239	74 149
Corporate direct taxes[1]	5 018	7 137	18 661	20 862	22 135	23 762	27 156
Other current taxes on income, wealth, etc.	353	621	976	1 623	1 694	1 872	1 952
Indirect taxes	15 908	31 667	48 710	62 843	66 804	70 803	73 412
Other current transfers received	152	437	879	1 570	1 766	1 924	2 142
Property income	2 604	6 533	7 209	11 316	13 564	12 813	13 711
Gross operating surplus	3 108	5 322	8 232	10 237	10 547	10 750	11 093
Gross income receivable	42 967	81 783	134 421	166 592	179 710	190 163	203 615
Subsidies	1 991	4 089	5 131	6 311	6 968	6 847	7 333
Social security outlays	9 272	17 518	27 100	41 896	45 370	46 241	46 817
Other current transfers paid	1 708	3 679	5 689	9 261	9 174	10 637	10 814
Interest on public debt	4 213	10 994	14 535	19 820	19 348	17 482	15 677
Gross income payable	17 184	36 280	52 455	77 288	80 860	81 207	80 641
Gross disposable income	25 784	45 501	81 965	89 304	98 852	108 957	122 975
Final consumption expenditure	25 879	48 399	73 701	92 843	96 885	100 256	104 784
Net saving[2]	–3 204	–8 220	31	–13 775	–8 580	–2 048	7 098
Consumption of fixed capital	3 108	5 322	8 232	10 237	10 547	10 750	11 093
Taxation[3] (per cent)							
Tax receipts (as a percentage of GDP)	28.4	30.0	30.6	30.4	31.1	30.3	
Personal income	12.5	13.6	13.1	12.3	12.8	12.8	
Corporate tax	3.5	2.8	4.3	4.5	4.7	4.3	
Payroll tax	1.4	1.4	1.9	2.1	2.1	2.0	
Tax on goods and services	8.8	9.9	8.5	8.9	8.7	8.6	
of which: Specific taxes on consumption	6.4	6.2	4.7	4.4	4.3	4.2	
Other Indicators							
Income tax as a percentage of total tax	44.0	45.2	43.0	40.5	41.2	42.2	
Net public debt as a percentage of GDP	..	..	11.0	27.8	22.3	22.4	17.0

	Prior to						After
Tax rates (per cent)	49		1st January 1990				47
Top rate of income tax	21		1st January 1991				20
Lower rate of income tax	33		1st July 1995				36
Corporate tax rate							

1. Including non-residents.
2. Net saving is derived as a balancing item.
3. Fiscal years.
Source: Australian Bureau of Statistics and OECD, *Revenue Statistics of OECD Member Countries.*

BASIC STATISTICS

BASIC STATISTICS:

INTERNATIONAL COMPARISONS

	Units	Reference period[1]	Australia	Austria
Population				
Total	Thousands	1997	18 532	8 072
Inhabitants per sq. km	Number	1997	2	96
Net average annual increase over previous 10 years	%	1997	1.3	0.6
Employment				
Total civilian employment (TCE)[2]	Thousands	1997	8 430	3 685
of which:				
Agriculture	% of TCE	1997	5.2	6.8
Industry	% of TCE	1997	22.1	30.3
Services	% of TCE	1997	72.7	63.8
Gross domestic product (GDP)				
At current prices and current exchange rates	Bill. US$	1997	392.9	206.2
Per capita	US$	1997	21 202	25 549
At current prices using current PPPs[3]	Bill. US$	1997	406.8	186.3
Per capita	US$	1997	21 949	23 077
Average annual volume growth over previous 5 years	%	1997	4.1	1.9
Gross fixed capital formation (GFCF)	% of GDP	1997	21.5	24.1
of which:				
Machinery and equipment	% of GDP	1997	10.3 (96)	8.8 (96)
Residential construction	% of GDP	1997	4.4 (96)	6.2 (96)
Average annual volume growth over previous 5 years	%	1997	7.3	2.8
Gross saving ratio[4]	% of GDP	1997	18.4	23
General government				
Current expenditure on goods and services	% of GDP	1997	16.7	19.4
Current disbursements[5]	% of GDP	1996	34.8	48
Current receipts	% of GDP	1996	35.4	47.9
Net official development assistance	% of GNP	1996	0.28	0.24
Indicators of living standards				
Private consumption per capita using current PPP's[3]	US$	1997	13 585	12 951
Passenger cars, per 1 000 inhabitants	Number	1995	477	447
Telephones, per 1 000 inhabitants	Number	1995	510	465
Television sets, per 1 000 inhabitants	Number	1994	489	480
Doctors, per 1 000 inhabitants	Number	1996	2.5	2.8
Infant mortality per 1 000 live births	Number	1996	5.8	5.1
Wages and prices (average annual increase over previous 5 years)				
Wages (earnings or rates according to availability)	%	1998	1.5	5.2
Consumer prices	%	1998	2.0	1.8
Foreign trade				
Exports of goods, fob*	Mill. US$	1998	55 882	61 754
As % of GDP	%	1997	15.6	28.4
Average annual increase over previous 5 years	%	1998	5.6	9
Imports of goods, cif*	Mill. US$	1998	60 821	68 014
As % of GDP	%	1997	15.3	31.4
Average annual increase over previous 5 years	%	1998	7.5	7
Total official reserves[6]	Mill. SDR's	1998	10 942	14 628 (97)
As ratio of average monthly imports of goods	Ratio	1998	2.2	2.7 (97)

* At current prices and exchange rates.
1. Unless otherwise stated.
2. According to the definitions used in OECD Labour Force Statistics.
3. PPPs = Purchasing Power Parities.
4. Gross saving = Gross national disposable income minus private and government consumption.

EMPLOYMENT OPPORTUNITIES

Economics Department, OECD

The Economics Department of the OECD offers challenging and rewarding opportunities to economists interested in applied policy analysis in an international environment. The Department's concerns extend across the entire field of economic policy analysis, both macro-economic and microeconomic. Its main task is to provide, for discussion by committees of senior officials from Member countries, documents and papers dealing with current policy concerns. Within this programme of work, three major responsibilities are:

- to prepare regular surveys of the economies of individual Member countries;
- to issue full twice-yearly reviews of the economic situation and prospects of the OECD countries in the context of world economic trends;
- to analyse specific policy issues in a medium-term context for the OECD as a whole, and to a lesser extent for the non-OECD countries.

The documents prepared for these purposes, together with much of the Department's other economic work, appear in published form in the *OECD Economic Outlook, OECD Economic Surveys, OECD Economic Studies* and the Department's *Working Papers* series.

The Department maintains a world econometric model, INTERLINK, which plays an important role in the preparation of the policy analyses and twice-yearly projections. The availability of extensive cross-country data bases and good computer resources facilitates comparative empirical analysis, much of which is incorporated into the model.

The Department is made up of about 80 professional economists from a variety of backgrounds and Member countries. Most projects are carried out by small teams and last from four to eighteen months. Within the Department, ideas and points of view are widely discussed; there is a lively professional interchange, and all professional staff have the opportunity to contribute actively to the programme of work.

Skills the Economics Department is looking for:

a) Solid competence in using the tools of both microeconomic and macroeconomic theory to answer policy questions. Experience indicates that this normally requires the equivalent of a Ph.D. in economics or substantial relevant professional experience to compensate for a lower degree.

b) Solid knowledge of economic statistics and quantitative methods; this includes how to identify data, estimate structural relationships, apply basic techniques of time series analysis, and test hypotheses. It is essential to be able to interpret results sensibly in an economic policy context.

c) A keen interest in and extensive knowledge of policy issues, economic developments and their political/social contexts.

d) Interest and experience in analysing questions posed by policy-makers and presenting the results to them effectively and judiciously. Thus, work experience in government agencies or policy research institutions is an advantage.

e) The ability to write clearly, effectively, and to the point. The OECD is a bilingual organisation with French and English as the official languages. Candidates must have excellent knowledge of one of these languages, and some knowledge of the other. Knowledge of other languages might also be an advantage for certain posts.

f) For some posts, expertise in a particular area may be important, but a successful candidate is expected to be able to work on a broader range of topics relevant to the work of the Department. Thus, except in rare cases, the Department does not recruit narrow specialists.

g) The Department works on a tight time schedule with strict deadlines. Moreover, much of the work in the Department is carried out in small groups. Thus, the ability to work with other economists from a variety of cultural and professional backgrounds, to supervise junior staff, and to produce work on time is important.

General information

The salary for recruits depends on educational and professional background. Positions carry a basic salary from FF 318 660 or FF 393 192 for Administrators (economists) and from FF 456 924 for Principal Administrators (senior economists). This may be supplemented by expatriation and/or family allowances, depending on nationality, residence and family situation. Initial appointments are for a fixed term of two to three years.

Vacancies are open to candidates from OECD Member countries. The Organisation seeks to maintain an appropriate balance between female and male staff and among nationals from Member countries.

For further information on employment opportunities in the Economics Department, contact:

Management Support Unit
Economics Department
OECD
2, rue André-Pascal
75775 PARIS CEDEX 16
FRANCE

E-Mail: eco.contact@oecd.org

Applications citing ''ECSUR'', together with a detailed *curriculum vitae* in English or French, should be sent to the Head of Personnel at the above address.

The Electronic Advantage
Ask for our free Catalogue

The Fast and Easy way to work with statistics and graphs!

- Cut and paste capabilities
- Quick search & find functions
- Zoom for magnifying graphics
- Uses ACROBAT software
  (included free of charge)
- Works on Windows

OECD on the WEB: **www.oecd.org**

Where to send your request:

In Austria, Germany and Switzerland

OECD Centre Bonn
August-Bebel-Allee 6,
D-53175 Bonn
Tel.: (49-228) 959 1215
Fax: (49-228) 959 1218
E-mail: bonn.contact@oecd.org
Internet: www.oecd.org/bonn

In Latin America

OECD Centre Mexico
Edificio INFOTEC
Av. San Fernando No. 37
Col. Toriello Guerra
Tlalpan C.P. 14050,
Mexico D.F.
Tel.: (52-5) 528 10 38
Fax: (52-5) 606 13 07
E-mail: mexico.contact@oecd.org
Internet: rtn.net.mx/ocde/

In the United States

OECD Center Washington
2001 L Street N.W., Suite 650
Washington, DC 20036-4922
Tel.: (202) 785 6323
Toll free: (1 800) 456-6323
Fax: (202) 785 0350
E-mail: washington.contact@oecd.org
Internet: www.oecdwash.org

In Asia

OECD Centre Tokyo
Landic Akasaka Bldg.
2-3-4 Akasaka, Minato-ku,
Tokyo 107-0052
Tel.: (81-3) 3586 2016
Fax: (81-3) 3584 7929
E-mail : center@oecdtokyo.org
Internet: www.oecdtokyo.org

In the rest of the world

OECD Paris Centre
2 rue André-Pascal, 75775 Paris Cedex 16, France
Fax: 33 (0)1 49 10 42 76 **Tel:** 33 (0)1 49 10 42 35
E-mail : sales@oecd.org
Internet : www.oecd.org
Online Orders: www.oecd.org/publications *(secure payment with credit card)*